PETITE RETREATS

PETITE RETREATS

Renewing Body, Mind, and Spirit

without Leaving Home

LINDA MASTRO
AND
ANNA HARDING

Library of Congress Control Number:		2006906812
ISBN 10:	Hardcover	1-4257-2664-X
	Softcover	1-4257-2663-1
ISBN 13:	Hardcover	978-1-4257-2664-5
	Softcover	978-1-4257-2663-8

Quote in Chapter One, The Heart of Petite Retreats, is from PLAN B: FURTHER THOUGHTS ON FAITH, copyright © 2005 by Anne Lamott. Used by permission of Riverhead Books, an imprint of Penguin Group (USA) Inc.

Quote in Chapter Ten, Shake Your Booty, used by permission of DAILY OM: THE DAILY SOURCE FOR NURTURING YOUR MIND, BODY & SPIRIT, copyright © 2004-06, www.dailyom.com.

Quote in Chapter Six, Queen of Sheba, is from the Practical Psychology column of Lloyd J. Thomas, Ph.D., life coach and licensed psychologist. Used by permission of Dr. Thomas, who publishes his columns through email subscription to PracticalPsychology-On@lists.webvalence.com.

This book was printed in the United States of America.

To order additional copies of this book, contact:
Xlibris Corporation
1-888-795-4274
www.Xlibris.com
Orders@Xlibris.com
34212

CONTENTS

For
Evelyn Boyce, my beloved Granny

For
Phoebe and Andre
and all my soul sisters

Acknowledgments

W hile our names grace the cover of this book, many people encouraged us as we gave birth to the concept of *Petite Retreats*.

Responses from the women whom we surveyed helped us respond to the needs they expressed when asked about their concept of a retreat. Thank you, Lainie Wrightson, Samantha McCall, Barbara Haddaway, and Frani Muth.

We received an outpouring of responses when we asked women to share ideas, books, music, videos, and other resources they rely on to restore their bodies, minds, and spirits. Their generosity helped us build a valuable reference section for this book. Our collaborators were Susan Delean-Botkin, Deborah Colborn, Susan duPont, Carol Gordean, Liz Watson, Laverne Webb, Phoebe Harding, Donnie Curran, Delpha Wright, Julia Moore, Suzanne Saussy, Brenda Stone, Melanie Maloney, Lee Nelson, Jeane Cockey, Susan Pyles, and Leslie Westbrook.

We applaud the dozens of women who attended our Petite Retreats workshops. While taking time to nurture themselves, they validated our belief that women crave time alone in their own homes.

Ann Swift and Phebe Barth graciously agreed to read our manuscript as we prepared it for publication. Their enthusiastic response and suggestions let us know that we were moving in the right direction.

Shawn Costello gave visual form to the spirit of *Petite Retreats*. Her inviting chair sketch appears in the book and inspired the oil painting beautifully transformed by Anne Hock for the cover. Lin Layton used her photographic genius to bring our faces to readers and to convert Anne's painting into digital format.

We extend our appreciation to Jeanne Pinault for her sharp eye and sage advice, which she offered with encouragement for our idea.

A deep bow of respect and love to Linda's husband, John Robinson, and her mother, Lorraine West. They both provided unwavering faith, financial support, and solitude throughout the creative process that birthed this book.

Much appreciation goes to Dedie King, Anna's first creative partner and close friend, who helped cultivate the seeds of *Petite Retreats* from a creative musing to a viable publishing venture.

We have undoubtedly omitted others who supported us and contributed to this creative journey. To all of you, we extend our gratitude.

Introduction

Who looks outside, dreams. Who looks inside, awakens.

—Carl Jung

What would you do if you magically discovered "free time" with nothing to do or no place to go? How would you spend the gift of a few hours or a whole day, alone, in your own home?

We invite you to experience a Petite Retreat.

This book is designed for women who long for time away from the routine . . . women who say,

> *I'd love a day to stay in my pajamas and read a book.*
> *I sure do miss digging in my garden.*
> *I wish I had time to finish organizing my sewing room.*
> *I could use some peace and quiet.*

The desire is strong but roadblocks seem even stronger . . .

> *I couldn't possibly leave the kids.*
> *I'd never get time off from work.*
> *My credit card is already maxed out.*
> *What on earth would I do with myself?*

Sound familiar?

ORIGINS OF *PETITE RETREATS*

The idea for this book emerged in 2004 during Anna's annual retreat. After completing a ten-day silent meditation retreat in Massachusetts, she visited friends, then took a solo journey north into Nova Scotia.

Driving with her thoughts uninterrupted by music or news, Anna traveled back roads that allowed her to enjoy the scenery at a slower pace. She began to ponder what had happened to her during her ten days of silence:

> *What was it about this annual experience that makes such a difference in my life?*
>
> *What were the essential ingredients that allow me to emerge with a mind less cluttered and more open to enjoying the small moments of my life?*
>
> *How can I create more of this type of experience without having to set aside a significant amount of time and money?*

Heading back home, Anna imagined the many people, women in particular, who want something similar in their lives. The idea of a Petite Retreat came into focus.

GIVE ME A BREAK

You can love your family, get a kick out of your work, and find satisfaction in your community projects. Yet even the most fulfilling life needs a break from an abundance of overdoing. At some point you need to unplug, get quiet, and reconnect with the woman everyone else finds so fascinating and competent.

Petite Retreats help cultivate a new attitude about your worth and a new relationship to your home. They are short chunks of time to tap into your yearnings, your wisdom, what you most want and value. With intention and permission, these home-based retreats can be habit-forming.

Reading this book and sampling some of the retreats will help you learn to have fun with the most important person in your life—YOU!

Ultimately, a Petite Retreat is all about intention. No matter what type of retreat you choose, this is your time, and how you spend it is completely determined by you—not your job, your family roles, or your list of "shoulds." A Petite Retreat is time alone with your inner Wise Woman, time to listen as she whispers—or maybe even shouts with attitude—what she needs in order to thrive, to be complete, to open to her essence.

Consider this an invitation to step away, to explore, to choose to be with your life in a different way.

THE JOURNEY INTO PETITE RETREATS

Just by opening this book you have begun your first Petite Retreat. The book will guide you into the kind of experience that only happens when you are alone, disconnected from the people and tasks that call you to accomplish or achieve. Your choices on how to use your special time are endless.

Taking a Petite Retreat requires giving yourself permission. Permission to step away from your never-ending list of commitments. Permission to rest, play, explore. And permission to make these small solo experiences a regular part of your routine.

This book is a guide that continually reinforces one of the basic premises of a Petite Retreat: It is all about you. You will have opportunities to reflect on questions that help you identify your needs, wants, and values. You can use the journal pages provided at the back of the book for these musings or buy yourself a special journal reserved just for your retreat experiences.

In **Chapter 1: The Heart of Petite Retreats,** you will find more information about Petite Retreats and the importance of not only doing them alone but doing them in your own home. Mindfulness is at the heart of Petite Retreats, calling you to pay attention whether you are doing the laundry, cooking a meal, dancing to your favorite song, or soaking in the tub.

Chapter 2: Getting Started will help you prepare for a Petite Retreat from the inside out. You will learn how to tap into your needs and set your intention for your retreat. You will come face to face with the obstacles that stand in your way—no time, no space, no money, no clue about what to do. Moving beyond the excuses, you will begin to explore some ideas for creating your retreat. This chapter also deals with the practical aspect of scheduling and preparation.

Chapter 3: Finding Your Bliss helps narrow down your choices. Here you will find exercises to help you identify what you most need and what type of retreat might best fill those needs. Perhaps your retreat time will be filled with a crafts project or cooking a sumptuous meal. Perhaps it will be a time of meditation and quiet reflection. You may nap, read, dance, or take a luxurious bath.

Chapters 4 through 11 offer details for Petite Retreats that nurture your body, stimulate your creativity, and cultivate your intellect. Others titillate your senses and mine the gold found in quiet contemplation. You will learn how cleaning out a closet or organizing old photographs can be relaxing and energizing. Each of these chapters outlines steps that will guide you to engage your mind, body, and environment for a few hours or a full day.

Chapter 12: Living Petite Retreats offers ideas for 5-, 15-, and 30-minute retreats that will help you continue to find solitude, rest, and renewal in your own home environment every day.

Chapter 13: Cooking Up a Petite Retreat gives you a recipe for designing your own retreats.

In the **Resources** section, you will find recommendations for books, music, videotapes, and websites that may enhance your Petite Retreat experience.

May your first Petite Retreat be a time of shameless enjoyment and secret indulgence. Try one retreat. Start small. Once you see that you only need as little as two hours and a few basic ingredients, we are confident that self-care will move to the top of your "To Do" list.

Your retreat has already begun. Take a breath. Turn the page. You deserve it.

Linda Mastro   *Anna Harding*

PART ONE

IT'S ALL ABOUT YOU

1

THE HEART OF PETITE RETREATS

I became more successful in my forties, but that pales in comparison with the other gifts of my current decade—how kind to myself I have become, what a wonderful, tender wife I am to myself, what a loving companion. I prepare myself tubs of hot water at the end of the day, and soak my tired feet. I run interference for myself when I am working, like the wife of a great artist would—"No, I'm sorry, she can't come. She's working hard these days, and needs a lot of down time." I live by the truth that "No" is a complete sentence. I rest as a spiritual act.
—Anne Lamott, *Plan B: Further Thoughts on Faith*

Petite Retreat. What do those two words suggest to you?

If you think that a retreat doesn't "count" unless you fly off to a spa in Hawaii, sequester yourself at a mountaintop monastery, or snuggle up in a secluded cabin for a week, then a Petite Retreat may seem like a strange concept.

So let's take a look at the elements of a Petite Retreat.

WHY KEEP IT PETITE?

Talking with our women friends and business associates about retreats, we heard them express longing and resistance. Although they ache for time to be quiet and restful, when they survey their busy lives, they conclude that adding one more thing, even something they desire and desperately need, is impossible.

Thus, the need for petite, as in a short period of time. Finding a week or even a weekend away for a retreat may be unrealistic for a busy mother or an active businesswoman. Retirees are scheduled months in advance with volunteer commitments and travel. Yet even the most overbooked woman can find a two-hour gap in her calendar.

One of the key components of a Petite Retreat is that it is short. And because the retreat is petite, you can easily transition back into your "normal life" feeling renewed and grateful.

In the chapters that guide you through Petite Retreat experiences, you will find suggestions for two kinds of retreat. The Short & Sweet retreat is designed to fill a two-hour time slot; the Full Course retreat can be scheduled for as few as four hours and as long as eight.

WHAT IS A RETREAT?

Women we asked described a retreat as . . .

- *Quiet time in spare surroundings*
- *To pull back from the day-to-day scheduling and create time to be by myself*
- *Time to rest, reflect, to do what I wish . . . thinking, reading or creating*
- *Peaceful relaxation and an opportunity for inspiration*
- *A time to restore the spirit away from the busy day-to-day world*
- *Solitude, quiet, reflection, nature, rest, deep listening, change of pace and perspective*
- *Meditation, simple food, rest*

Their answers suggest that women turn to retreats for simplicity, solitude, and freedom.

One woman referred to a retreat as "Back to the womb." Take a moment and imagine that: No responsibilities. Alone but supported. Active and growing.

The womb experience ended with a traumatic push into life. And many women have been pushing ever since.

In its most general definition, a retreat is a withdrawing or stepping away. A retreat is an opportunity to slow down and get a broader perspective. Sometimes you need to get outside of your daily routine to see what you really want from life. If you are having trouble imagining a life that is more healthy, more fulfilling, more you, a Petite Retreat may be the perfect place to begin.

HOME ALONE

A Petite Retreat has two important aspects that make it different from other kinds of retreats. You take the retreat alone and you stay at home.

We got mixed responses when we asked women, *"Could* you do a short retreat in your own home?"

Some said, "Absolutely!" and were excited about time to enjoy their homes without interruption. Others anticipated difficulties. They wondered how they could ask spouses, roommates, and children to leave. Undone chores could be a distraction.

Taking a retreat in your home requires a shift in perspective. Instead of seeing it as just one more workplace, the place where you live becomes the setting for rest and renewal. If home is, indeed, where the heart is, then an at-home retreat provides an opportunity to reconnect with your innermost longings.

You may need to close a door on a messy room or drape a pile of clutter with a pretty scarf. Answering machines can handle the phone. Laundry can wait. Ask a friend to take the kids, just for a couple of hours.

Because a Petite Retreat is done at home, you learn to associate the restful and nourishing qualities and inspirations experienced during your retreat with your most intimate environment. You begin to see your home in a different light. Each retreat recharges you—and your home—with renewed energy that you can draw on long after the retreat is over.

One woman admitted that the idea of being home alone *"makes me anxious."* For many people the experience of being alone for any period of time is both rare and unsettling. Phones, radios, television, and computers are sources of entertainment and distraction at work and at home. Staying so connected may prevent you from venturing into the landscape of your interior world.

In times of stress and overwhelm, living alone on a desert island may seem like the perfect escape for some women. For others, the reality of even just a few hours alone induces fear. You may imagine feeling lonely, insecure, and uncomfortable when you unplug from the structure and frenzy that shapes your life. For single women who live on their own, the prospect of more alone time may hold little appeal.

Once you develop the skill of being alone and know how and when to use it, you may find that you are more centered and self-sufficient, no matter what life hands you. Being alone does not mean being lonely. In fact, reframing alone as "all one" may make it possible for you to more easily connect with the whole you. When you get quiet, your inner Wise Woman can speak to you softly in a voice that cannot be heard over the din of daily life.

If the prospect of being alone makes you feel uneasy, you may be receiving a signal that life is calling you to take a risk and try something new. One woman expressed this mix of discomfort and excitement when contemplating taking a retreat at home:

> I would find it difficult because being in my usual surroundings, not doing anything, would feel strange. I'm not sure how comfortable it would be. However, it also sounds like an amazing experience and one I'd be intrigued to try.

Look at a Petite Retreat as a small step toward enjoying your own company. Undefined by roles, activities, and responsibilities, even for a short period, you may learn things that will enrich your life in ways you cannot yet imagine.

MINDFULLY YOURS

Mindfulness is at the core of a Petite Retreat. The concept of mindfulness is often linked to meditation—the act of being fully present to the here and now. In fact, meditation is just one pathway to mindfulness. At its heart, the practice is about paying attention on purpose, whether you are doing the laundry, cooking a meal, dancing to your favorite song, or soaking in the tub.

Silence is another key component of a Petite Retreat. Unless you sing or talk to yourself or your pets, being alone will mean not speaking for the duration of your retreat. Take a minute and consider this. What feelings come up when you think about not talking to another person for two hours or a whole day? You may take a deep breath and sigh with delicious anticipation. You might wonder, "What would that be like?"

When you approach situations mindfully, you notice and observe without judgment or interpretation. Instead of making up stories about the phenomena around you, you absorb yourself in the experience, awake to its colors, sounds, tastes, and feelings. In this state of mind, a thought or a bodily sensation is as interesting—and as fleeting—as a butterfly that lights for a moment then flutters away. Mindfulness requires being aware and attentive to each moment. Without expectations, you open to questions and insights as they arise.

Approaching a Petite Retreat as an exercise in mindfulness is an opportunity to see your surroundings in a new light. You also get a glimpse into your inner world and the dreams and delights that make you feel alive.

Even if taking time for yourself is something you do regularly, you can move into a Petite Retreat as a practice in mindfully reconnecting with your heart and your home.

————————————

To summarize,

A Petite Retreat is a short time at home alone, a time to listen and respond to your heart's desire for simplicity, solitude, and freedom.

A Petite Retreat reframes your home as a welcoming nest, where you can rest and renew.

A Petite Retreat is an opportunity to practice mindfulness, so that you are aware of sensations, thoughts, and feelings that accompany your experience.

Ready to get started? Let's go!

2

GETTING STARTED

Twenty years from now you will be more disappointed by the things you didn't do than by the ones you did do. So throw off the bowlines. Sail away from the safe harbor. Catch the trade winds in your sails. Explore. Dream. Discover.

—Mark Twain

Special occasions require planning so that every detail is in order when the big event arrives. People shop and bake for months preparing for holiday feasts. As soon as a party invitation arrives in the mail, you may start planning what to wear and wondering who else will be there.

Once you have decided to take a Petite Retreat, some advanced preparation will ensure that you arrive at your scheduled time with everything you need—supplies, space, and privacy. Instead of skidding breathlessly into your retreat, you can let yourself relax into the experience.

BEGIN WITH INTENTION

The foundation of a Petite Retreat is the attitude with which you approach this time alone in your home. By answering these questions, you set the tone for each retreat:

What do I want from my Petite Retreat?
How do I want to feel when my retreat is over?

Answers may come slowly at first, particularly if you live your life focused on the wants and needs of others. Before you start working out the details of what you will do and for how long, sit with these questions. Take some time to let your reactions surprise you. Then make a few notes about whatever comes up.

Your answers will lead you to the intention for your retreat. Intention gives focus to your time. The more clarity you have about what you want, the more likely you are to get it.

Intention is a statement of purpose that will help you decide what type of retreat you want to pursue and how to use your time. Defining what you need, what you want, and the feelings you want to evoke before your retreat begins will keep you focused once you arrive. If you are tempted to throw in a load of laundry or check your e-mail, your intention will draw you back to the reason you scheduled the retreat.

Your intention statement consists of what you intend to experience and how you want to feel when it is over. For example, you might write,

On my Petite Retreat I intend to focus on extreme self-care by pampering myself in ways I overlook during my busy schedule. When my retreat is over I want to feel relaxed, soft, and refreshed.

Here are a few more examples:

I want to re-energize my body through movement and healthy food. When my retreat is over I want to feel alive, renewed and invigorated.
I want to reconnect with my childlike sense of creativity and fun. When my retreat is over I want to feel satisfied, playful and inspired.
I want to challenge myself to think and act 'out of the box.' When my retreat is over I want to feel expanded, proud and courageous.

Your intention statement may be longer or shorter. You will know it is complete when reading it out loud gives you goose bumps or a feeling of excitement. An intention statement is on target when it makes you sit back and say, "Yes, that is what I want!"

YES, BUT . . . NO MORE EXCUSES

After a few minutes of savoring the possibility of your Petite Retreat, excuses may start to whisper in your ear.

A Petite Retreat sounds just like what I need, but . . .

- *I don't have a free minute for the next three months.*
- *I'll take a Petite Retreat after I clean my closets, paint the bedroom, weed the garden, balance my checkbook . . .*
- *I don't have anyone to watch my kids* (or Dad, or anyone else who depends on your care).
- *My husband would never understand.*
- *It seems selfish to want some time alone when I already spend so much time away from my family.*
- *I wouldn't know what to do with my time.*

Let's address the last excuse first. Just a few pages away are suggested retreat activities in a variety of "flavors." You can follow the suggested retreats step-by-step or use them as a guide for designing something uniquely your own.

The number one excuse women list is lack of time. Before you can find a chunk of time in your date book, you may need to face some unconscious roadblocks, excuses founded on untested assumptions. Excuses are often assumptions that, when challenged, hold no truth. Looking with a more open mind may help dispel a faulty assumption.

Consider your concern about finding someone to take care of your children or a dependent parent. That young couple down the street might like to test drive parenthood by taking your son to the zoo. Your friend whose father just passed away might enjoy an afternoon reminiscing with your Dad. Perhaps the parents of one of your child's friends will host a play date while you take your retreat. One day, you may be able to return the favor when your neighbor, mother, or friend decides to take her own Petite Retreat.

If your husband or partner seems like an obstacle, check it out. Discuss your idea of an at-home retreat and request the time and privacy you need. You won't get what you need unless you ask.

You may find that the biggest hurdle you have to overcome is your own belief that you can only take a break after you complete everything on your "To Do" list. If your desire for a Petite Retreat is met with *"I can't because . . . ," "I won't unless . . . ,"* or *"I'd better not until . . . ,"* you may have to step back and take stock. You may find that reserving time for a Petite Retreat will recharge you so that you can make headway on projects you shelved because you were too tired or overwhelmed.

Another obstacle to scheduling time for yourself is the echo of a voice from your childhood that instructs, "Don't be selfish!" If you learned early in life that making other people happy was part of the formula for being a "good girl," you may need to learn to distinguish between being selfish and being "self" centered in a healthy way. Think of it this way: Being selfish means taking care of yourself to the exclusion of everyone around you. "My way or the highway" thinking is alienating and ultimately destructive to your relationships. Being centered *in* your self, in your own values and aspirations, on the other hand, is only giving yourself the respect that you readily give to others. A healthy sense of self enables you to take a deep and long look inside, finding what you value and giving yourself what you need.

Take a few minutes and see what surfaces when you consider:

> *What is keeping me from taking this step into self-care?*
> *How can I give myself permission to schedule just two hours for me?*
> *What prevents me from feeling that I deserve this gift?*

Exercise: Shifting from Excuses to Permission

- Make a list of all of the excuses that prevent you from scheduling a Petite Retreat.
- Next to each item, add one suggestion for how you can eliminate this perceived obstacle.
- Let this be an exercise in creativity. One by one, take down the barriers.

Remember to call in support from your family and friends. Let them know how important this is to you. Who knows, you may inspire them to do the same thing for themselves!

MAKING PREPARATIONS

In her 1929 essay "A Room of One's Own," Virginia Woolf claimed that women authors need their own money and their own room to write. Almost eighty years later, women are more likely to achieve financial independence than they are to find a private space in their own homes.

The solution may be in redefining what a room of your own looks like. You may never take a Petite Retreat if you wait to save money for an addition to your home or count the years for a child to leave home so you can convert her room into your special nook.

The type of retreat you take will determine the kind of space you will need. Space consists not only of the physical area in which you will experience your retreat, but also all of the "ingredients" you will need for your selected activities

Each of the sample retreats in this book includes ideas for how to prepare for your retreat. You will find suggestions for how to clear a space in your home and for specific items you might need to collect, borrow or purchase.

In addition to the ideas listed for each retreat, for all Petite Retreats eliminate distractions by making these basic preparations:

- Request as much space as you need. Ask your housemates to find somewhere else to spend the hours you have set aside for your retreat. If they cannot leave the house, identify the space you will be using—your bedroom, the kitchen, a bathroom—and ask them to respect your privacy.
- Let everyone who might need to contact you during your retreat know that you will be unavailable for the time you have blocked off.
- Unplug the phone or turn down the ringer so the answering machine can take your messages. Turn off your cell phone and pager.
- Avoid checking your e-mail or mindlessly surfing the Internet.
- Unless you are watching a video or DVD as one of your retreat activities, turn off the TV.
- Make a list of everything you will need—food, water, beverages, books, art supplies, clothes, music. Shop or run errands ahead of time to avoid running out for any missing ingredients.
- Consult the **Resources** section of this book for reading, music, and video suggestions that may enhance your retreat plan.
- Set a timer so that you can avoid watching the clock.

INVOKING THE SPIRIT OF PETITE RETREAT

Important gatherings often begin with a ritual. The chairman bangs a gavel to call a meeting to order. Church bells sound the beginning of a service. Applause welcomes the maestro onto the concert stage.

A Petite Retreat begins and ends with a candle lighting ritual. For centuries, people have used candles as more than sources of light. Spiritual rituals of all denominations incorporate some form of candle lighting to signal that something sacred is about to unfold.

Think about the candle's flame as a symbol of your inner light. Use the candle as a focal point, something to draw you back into the intention of your retreat. The ordinary becomes extraordinary through this symbolic gesture of illumination.

You may want to make an altar on which to display your candle. An altar serves as a reminder of the link between the spiritual and material worlds. The presence of an altar symbolizes that what happens in a space has personal and spiritual significance.

In chapter 4, **Stepping into Stillness**, you will find directions for building your own at-home altar. Your altar may consist of a few items that represent your intention—a photograph of a loved one, a postcard from a place that evokes feelings of relaxation, flowers, incense, sea shells collected on a memorable vacation, a book of poetry. The list is personal and endless.

TAKING NOTE

In *The Artist's Way*, Julia Cameron presents a technique that she calls the morning pages. A form of journaling, this process entails writing three longhand pages each morning to tap into your fears, questions, gripes, and joys. Cameron says, "The pages are a pathway to a strong and clear sense of self. They are a trail that we follow into our own interior, where we meet both our own creativity and our creator."

Journaling is the process of listening to and recording your thoughts. Just as meditation and daydreaming give you insights into your internal life, journaling is a doorway into what you want, the obstacles you face, and ideas for breaking through to creative solutions.

Each retreat featured in this book includes questions to stimulate reflection. Specific questions help develop your intention before a retreat; others are designed to process the experience when it is over. Throughout a retreat, you may want to make notes about what you are experiencing. Journaling gives form to your thoughts, feelings, questions, and actions. Your retreat reflections can be a valuable resource for tracking changes in your life and for making plans for your next retreat.

Journaling requires no special skills or materials. You may want to invest in a notebook that will be dedicated to your Petite Retreat musings. An old-fashioned copybook or spiral-bound tablet will do the job. Treat yourself to some colored pens to give journaling a more playful tone.

BOOKING A RESERVATION

The final step in your preparation is setting a date. Get out your calendar and review your schedule for the next thirty days. Find a chunk of time when you can schedule your Petite Retreat. Find an afternoon, an evening, a weekend morning—then write "Petite Retreat" in ink in your date book.

Is every weekday, evening, and weekend booked for months ahead? Consider taking a midnight retreat. The quiet hours in the middle of the night might be a perfect time to read a novel or to gaze at the stars.

Your Petite Retreat date is sacred time. Give it the same importance as a dental appointment or a meeting with your child's teacher. If someone asks you to meet them for lunch, help with a project, or go shopping, look at the slot on your calendar and say, "No, thanks. I have plans."

3

FINDING YOUR BLISS

Be yourself; no base imitator of another, but your best self. There is something which you can do better than another. Listen to the inward voice and bravely obey that.

—Ralph Waldo Emerson

Many of the women we talked to knew exactly how they would spend their Petite Retreat time. Some said they needed guidance, a laundry list of ideas to spark their imagination. Others wanted step-by-step instructions.

The following chapters offer suggestions and instructions for short and longer retreats in a variety of "flavors."

You might ask, "How do I know which retreat to choose?"

As your read on, you will find a list of questions to help you decide. The questions prompt you to discover what you need right now. You can return to this list over and over, not only to pick a retreat theme, but also to check in with the state of your emotional, physical, intellectual, and creative health.

CHECKING IN

Set some time aside for this part of the Petite Retreat planning process. Just as you will schedule a block of time for the retreat, mark your calendar "Finding My Bliss" to give yourself an opportunity to complete this exercise prior to the date of your retreat.

You may want to do this all at one time—sit for an hour or more to explore all of the following questions. You can also make this a daily exercise over some period of time. Take a few minutes every morning or before you go to bed to explore a question and listen for answers.

However you decide to approach the checking in process, use your journal to make notes. The insights that surface will be valuable guides as you browse through the sample retreats to find the one that best fits your mood and interests. Be open to surprises.

The Questions

- *What is missing in my life?*
- *What do I have too much of in my life?*
- *What is a feeling I yearn for that I haven't felt in a long time? What emotions do I long to experience—happiness, contentment, fulfillment? How do I want to feel at the end of my retreat?*
- *What part of me hasn't been expressed lately?*
- *If I could accomplish one small thing that would make me feel more alive, satisfied, and healthy, what would it be?*
- *What did I once do for fun that I don't do now?*
- *What have I always wanted to attempt but have been too scared to try?*
- *What activities do I keep putting off for lack of time?*
- *What do my body, mind, and spirit need?*

  - o *Is my body craving self-care, activity, movement, rest?*
  - o *Does my mind want spaciousness, quiet, stimulation, entertainment?*
  - o *Is my spirit calling me to be introspective, present, playful, simple?*

- *What is my current relationship with my home? What shifts would I like to make so that my home feels like a nurturing, stimulating, restful place?*
- *How does the season reflect what I need? Do the weather, food, and other elements suggest ideas for how I can meet my needs?*

Look back over your journal notes. Using your answers, take a few minutes to fill in the blanks of the following statements. Let your imagination soar. List activities, projects, interests that call to you now that you have a better appreciation for how you want to feel and what you need.

If I had two hours to enjoy myself I would . . .
If I had a whole day to enjoy myself I would . . .

JUST A TASTE OR A FULL MEAL?

Each retreat chapter offers ideas for two retreats. The Short & Sweet retreat is designed for two hours; the Full Course retreat can fill up a full day. "Day" is loosely defined as eight hours, and can begin when you wake up in the morning or in the evening when the rest of the world goes to sleep.

You may be tempted to jump right into one of the longer retreats. Be realistic. If you find that reserving a full day means you will have to wait months before you can take a Petite Retreat, find a two-hour time slot. Small steps taken often can be more satisfying than the occasional grand leap.

ORDERING FROM THE MENU

You now have a sense of your needs and of the time you can set aside. In the following chapters you will find a buffet of choices to satisfy many different Petite Retreat appetites.

Stepping into Stillness: Meditation in its many forms shapes this retreat. Sit, walk, chant, breathe your way into the core of your being. Feel *quiet, contemplative, prayerful, aware, introspective, receptive.*

Come to Your Senses: Stop to smell the roses, taste the fruit, see the flowers . . . you get the idea. Revel in the sights, sounds, feel of your body, your home, your life. Feel *stimulated, appreciative, awake, amazed, renewed, connected.*

Queen of Sheba: This at-home spa experience is a decadent immersion into a long soak in the tub accompanied by a facial, manicure, pedicure, and foot massage. Feel *pampered, sensual, relaxed, nurtured.*

Evoking the Muse: Play is the foundation of this retreat. Creativity is the doorway to fun and inspiration. Feel *expressed, playful, excited, focused, grateful.*

Two Thumbs Up: Sit back and be entertained. Pick your genre—books, magazines, movies, music, games. Feel *joyful, inspired, awed, delighted, silly, engaged, carefree.*

Just Doing It: Making headway on a project can be a most satisfying way to spend time alone. Dip into your "To Do" list for ideas that will revitalize your relationship with your home and with yourself. Feel *accomplished, satisfied, proud, relieved, competent.*

Shake Your Booty: This retreat revolves around body movement and awareness. Use this retreat to jump-start an exercise program or reconnect with how your body feels when it dances and stretches. Be in your own skin. Feel *invigorated, energized, rejuvenated, appreciative.*

Risky Business: Try something new, stretch yourself, daydream. Step out of the box and into your life. Feel *expanded, stretched, titillated, edgy, adventurous.*

PLANNING VS. SPONTANEITY

The women who told us about their retreat fantasies had mixed feelings about creating a retreat plan.

One woman said, "I like to plan sometimes, but the most special times for me are the ones that just unfold and perhaps come as surprises, like when something I've planned gets cancelled and I have a gift of time."

Another said, "I know that I would like to plan it and give myself an outline of what I would be doing. I just think knowing the time is set, and there is a specific goal to accomplish within that time, would be a good thing for me."

Consider your style. Use the retreats offered in the following chapters as a guide. Try them out as designed or mix and match the parts that draw you in. Remember: A Petite Retreat is all about YOU.

PART TWO

THE RETREATS

4

STEPPING INTO STILLNESS

In the attitude of silence the soul finds the path in a clearer light, and what is elusive and deceptive resolves itself into crystal clearness.
—Mahatma Gandhi

Stillness is an uncommon state for most busy women. Falling into bed at the end of a day may be as close as you come to stillness on a normal day. Even then, though, you may toss and turn with dreams and wake up with an endless list of unfinished business scrolling through your head.

In this retreat, you will experience stillness as a state of mind and of body. Stillness becomes an opportunity to cultivate awareness of the thoughts and feelings bubbling under the surface.

A Stepping into Stillness Petite Retreat is time to cultivate mindfulness—paying attention on purpose. In a couple of hours or a full day, you examine behaviors and beliefs that seem so real and so true, until subjected to the microscope of attention. Practicing awareness brings you into contact with what Eckhart Tolle calls "the power of now." And in that place, you begin to develop compassion—for yourself, for the people with whom you share your life, for all beings—while also building spiritual muscles that will guide you through life's more turbulent waters.

SETTING YOUR INTENTION

What do I want from a Stepping into Stillness retreat?

The first step is to put aside any goals or expectations. There is no right or wrong. Paying attention is the cost of admission and the reward is hearing, perhaps for the first time, what many spiritual teachers call the "still, small voice within." Perhaps you have been grappling with a question about your work, a relationship, your health, or some other aspect of your life. Bring one of these questions to your retreat and listen to what wisdom emerges when you give yourself permission to practice stillness.

If your life is a never-ending series of meetings, chores, projects, and tending to the needs of others, this retreat is a way to pull the plug on these activities, no matter how rewarding they may be. Slowing down, going inward, truly stepping into another dimension of what life can offer . . . these are all possibilities if you just give yourself permission to practice meditative awareness.

In a sentence or two, record in your journal:

> *What I want most to experience during my Stepping into Stillness retreat is . . .*

Now consider:

> *How do I want to feel at the end of my Petite Retreat?*

Pick two or three words to describe how you would like to feel after experiencing a few hours of solitude and silence. Some ideas . . . *centered, peaceful, attuned, alive, curious, amazed, focused, aware, awake, grateful.*

In your journal write:

> *At the end of my Stepping into Stillness retreat, I want to feel . . .*

MAKING PREPARATIONS

During the Short & Sweet retreat you will be creating a home altar. The Full Course retreat builds on the short retreat by adding instructions for several meditation practices that you will sample along with mindfully preparing a meal.

To prepare for your retreat, you will need to do some advance preparation. Here are some things to consider doing ahead of time:

- For a longer retreat find a recipe for a meal and stock up on the ingredients and equipment required to prepare a special feast.
- Find a space where you can set up an altar. This may require some negotiation if you share your home with family or a roommate. If you have several spaces, use your intuition to pick the right one. Walk slowly through the house and notice how you respond to the environment of each area. Open your mind to a creative solution, such as converting a bookshelf to a small altar area, or a "junk" closet into a special nook. If space for a permanent altar is not available, find a cigar box, a tray, or a basket that you can use to make a mobile altar. Once you have found a location for your altar, clear it of any dirt and clutter.
- Begin to gather items with which to build your altar. Ideas can include: candles; incense; photos of loved ones; sacred statues; special stones or rocks; seashells from your favorite beach; beads; decorative fabric; inspirational books; a bell, rattle, chime, singing bowl or a tingsha; gemstones such as amethyst, aventurine, rose quartz, jasper, and clear crystal
- You may want to read *Altars as Icons: Sacred Spaces in Everyday Life* by Jean McMann listed in the **Resources** section. Visit a church, take a walk in the woods, or browse in a specialty shop to get other ideas for your altar.

INGREDIENTS FOR THIS RETREAT

- Meditation cushion [NOTE: You can make your own cushion with stacks of comfy pillows or by folding blankets into a padded seat.]
- Timer
- Ingredients to prepare a meal
- Objects for your altar

THE RETREAT COMMENCES

For both the short and full-day retreats, after you have set your intention, light your Petite Retreat candle and say,

> *As I light this candle, I commit to creating a time for myself in which I find renewal and enjoyment. During my Petite Retreat, I intend to* [restate the intention you recorded in your journal.]

Sit for a few minutes and let your intention start to simmer.

SHORT & SWEET RETREAT: Altar-ed States

In this two-hour retreat, you will be creating an altar. Traditionally, altars have been the centerpiece for sacred worship. They are often adorned with candles, statues, holy books, and other religious objects. Although the home altar may look more secular, even playful, it is meant to be a spiritual touchstone, a place to remember the sacred at the heart of your life. No matter how big or small, how elaborately decorated or simple, an altar is a place that acknowledges the connection between your inner and outer lives.

If the idea of bringing an altar into your home feels out of sync with your normal way of living, consider the collections or special items displayed that already exist in your home. Do you put up a tree at Christmas? How about your mantel—is it covered with framed photos of friends and loved ones? Take a look at your refrigerator—is it decorated with a child's artwork and magnets with inspirational, even irreverent, sayings? The bulletin board over your desk may be covered with postcards from around they world. In their own way, these are all altars. They remind you of the people whom you love, the places that delight you, the magnificence and joys of the everyday.

The altar you create during this retreat becomes the focal point of this and all of the other Petite Retreats you will take. It can be the place where you light your candle at the beginning of each retreat, where you sit and journal, and where you plan your next retreat. Your altar may be stationary, set in a specific corner of a room that is all your own; it can be mobile, tucked in a small box or basket or set on a tray that you can move from place to place. The format is less important than the intention and spirit that infuses your creation.

The experience of building your altar becomes a meditation when you pay close attention to its many elements—location, contents, size, colors, textures. Focus on process—selecting the items and how you arrange them—more than on what the finished product will look like. At the outset, know that your altar is organic and, like your life, it will evolve. This will free you to create with the same attitude used by the Tibetan monks who build elaborate sand mandalas and, when the design is complete, sweep it away to symbolize the impermanence of all things, no matter how precious.

Designing from the Inside Out

Before you start filling up the space with random objects, take a few minutes to reflect on these questions and make some notes in your journal:

> *What do I want more of in my life?* Consider what is missing or in
> short supply. Some ideas may include compassion, courage, quiet, focus,
> calm, flexibility, balance, energy, lightness, fun.

Who or what represents the feelings or attributes I want more of in my life? Perhaps there is a person whom you admire, maybe a renowned spiritual leader, such as the Dalai Lama, a saint or god-figure. You might see what you want more of in your pet, your child, a parent, a friend. Nature may be a source of inspiration—a tree that has grown despite losing a branch to a snow storm, the resilience of spring daffodils, an intricately marked seashell.

What colors evoke the feelings and attributes I want more of in my life? Bright, primary colors may give you clarity and energy. The seven chakra colors may hold special meaning. Stark white may represent open-mindedness and freedom.

What textures evoke the feelings and attributes I want more of in my life? Sensuous silk, knotty wood, sturdy clay, delicate glass—what tactile sensations soothe and center you?

Sit with your notes and the images that came up during this exercise. Look for themes and recurring images. What you discover will guide you to build an altar that it is a reflection of your inner desires and joys.

How you decorate your altar is limited only by your imagination. In *Altars as Icons: Sacred Spaces in Everyday Life*, Jean McMann says, "[A] material thing—a stone, a photograph, an old shoe—can become a shrine when it is displayed in a way that evokes inspiration, memory, respect or reverence."

A silk scarf for an altar cloth and a simple white candle may symbolize the simplicity you are seeking. Bird feathers, a sprig of budding forsythia and a book of poetry may call you back to the flight and fancy of nature. With a string of rosary beads, a statue of the Virgin Mary and a stick of burning incense, you can relive the mystical reverence of attending Sunday Mass as a young girl.

You may select a couple of objects as the focal point of your altar. They will set the tone and ensure that what you add has meaning. Tease and please your senses with your altar objects. Bring in scents with candles, incense, sage, and flowers. Treat yourself to a bell or a Tibetan tingsha to add sound to your sacred space.

Be sure that you will be comfortable while you sit with your altar. Some people like sitting on the floor on a specially designed meditation cushion or bench. You may prefer a straight-backed chair in which you can sit with your feet on the floor and your spine supported. Keep a silk shawl or a hand-knitted afghan nearby to keep you warm and remind you that you are in a nurturing place.

When you have arranged your items on your altar, sit for a few minutes. Soak in what you see. Close your eyes and know that all of the attributes represented on your altar already exist deep within your heart. Return to your altar whenever you need to check in and access your inner qualities and dreams.

Keeping It Sacred

Just like other aspects of your home, an altar needs regular maintenance. Cleaning your altar becomes another form of mindfulness when you take time to stop and see each item anew.

Several times a year, take everything off your altar and reevaluate each piece. If something has gotten torn, has faded, or no longer has significance, remove it. If your altar has gotten overgrown, weed out unnecessary cards, poems, photos, and other items that have outlived their usefulness. Repeat the journal exercise you did when you first created your altar to see if your needs have changed and what types of items and images might better support you.

FULL COURSE RETREAT: A Meditation Sampler

This longer Stepping into Stillness retreat builds on the Short & Sweet retreat by adding a meditation sampler. Whether you are an experienced meditator or someone unpracticed at sitting still doing nothing, this retreat is an opportunity to step out of well-worn patterns into a more contemplative, reflective frame of mind.

The Full Course retreat revolves around several meditation practices. The word "practice" is used deliberately to dispel any expectations that you have to get it right the first time or ever. There is no right or wrong way, time, place, position, or accessories that will magically transform you into an enlightened being (if only it were so!) The practice is to show up, be still, pay attention.

During your Stepping into Stillness retreat, the concept of stillness means more than lack of movement. Stillness connotes awareness that comes from being fully present. As you cook, walk, build an altar, and move through this retreat, consider yourself as a still point from which you view the world around you, observing with curiosity the feelings, thoughts, and questions that arise.

Seated Meditation

Throughout the Full Course retreat, you will be taking short, seated meditation breaks. The purpose of these pauses is to reflect and digest the previous activity and to bring you back to a still, centered place of non-doing.

Although you will be guided to sit for ten minutes, meditate for shorter or longer periods depending on your comfort level.

Use the following seated meditation guide to begin your Stepping into Stillness retreat. You can return to these instructions when a **Reflection** break is suggested.

> **Tip:** Set a timer for the length of your seated meditation so that you can avoid looking at your watch or worrying about how long you have been sitting.

- Find a comfortable seated position. You can sit in a chair, preferably one in which your spine will be straight and the soles of your feet can easily touch the floor. If you prefer, sit on the floor cross-legged on a cushion or on a meditation bench.
- Sit with your back straight and relaxed. Let the muscles of the rest of your body soften and relax. Rest your hands on your knees or in your lap.
- Close your eyes and take a breath. Consciously look for tension in your face, neck, arms, feet, and stomach and let the muscles release. Feel the sensation of your breath as it enters your nostrils. As you breathe in, you might notice, "cool." As you breath out you might notice, "warm." Feel how your chest and belly expand with the inhalation and contract with the exhalation. Even in stillness, much is happening in your body.
- As you breathe normally, pick a focus point. You can point your attention to the temperature of the breath or the movement of breath as it comes in and goes out. Train your awareness to notice the first moment of the in-breath. Sustain the attention for the duration of just that one in-breath. When you need to exhale, notice the out-breath and how it is slightly different from the in-breath.
- Thoughts and feelings will arise as you attempt to focus on your breath. This is the way the mind works. It is a busy place! Patiently label the thoughts "Thinking," then bring your awareness back to the breath. Treat the wandering mind as you would a playful puppy excited about everything it sees, hears, and smells. Call it back lovingly as a patient teacher, not an exacting judge.
- Your meditation will be an exercise in building awareness. As you breathe, thoughts will vie for your attention. Notice when you have strayed from focusing on the breath to following a thought. Remember: Meditation is all about gently bringing yourself back to the breath and letting go of the thoughts that distract you. You might do this a hundred times in a short sitting: *A trip to the Bahamas.* Come back to the breath. *A conversation you want to have with a friend.* Come back to the breath. *A pain in your knee from sitting still for so long.* Come back to the breath.
- When the timer chimes the end of your seated meditation, slowly open your eyes. Stretch, wiggle, bringing movement back into your body. Look around and notice the room. Feel your body and note the state of your mind. You may want to make a few notes in your journal.

Altar-ed States

If you have not already made an altar, take the next couple of hours for this activity. [Follow the instructions for the Short & Sweet retreat.]

If you have an altar, take time to review every item. Take it off the altar, touch it, clean it, evaluate if it still inspires and pleases you. Discard or move anything that has served its purpose and add a new item.

When you have completed making your altar or rejuvenating your existing sacred space, take a short seated meditation break.

A Mindful Meal

At some point in your Full Course retreat, when you are hungry, preparing a meal is an exercise in mindfulness. Let what is often a mundane chore become an awe-inspiring connection with the process of nourishing your body, mind, and spirit.

Just as focusing on your breath is a way to stay aware during seated meditation, your senses will serve the same purpose for this cooking meditation.

Gather the ingredients you need for the recipes you selected. Step back and observe the colors and the shapes. Pick up each item and feel its weight in your hand. Touch the surfaces and feel their textures. Smell the herbs and produce. Imagine how they looked when they were still growing on the vine or bush, sun and rain nurturing their growth.

When you begin cooking, watch how these ingredients change. When you slice or chop a vegetable, look at its inside shapes and patterns. Smell the heating oil and notice how it brings out the scents of the vegetables, spices, and sauces. Listen as the food sizzles and sautés. Breathe in the aromas. Observe each ingredient, each step of the cooking process. Move slowly.

Fully experience each step of the preparation. Take your time. Nibble with slow, mindful bites as the food cooks.

When you come to a break in your cooking, set your table. Make this a ritual of self-care, using the same attention you would give a valued guest. Bring out your best dinnerware. Notice its patterns and colors, remembering the joy you experienced when you made this purchase or accepted this gift. Rub your hand over the plate. See your reflection in the handle of the silverware. Add a vase of flowers and some candles.

When your food is ready, arrange each item on your plate, paying special attention to how the colors complement one another. Watch the steam rise from the plate as the aromas mingle. Pour yourself a beverage.

At the table, sit quietly before you take the first bite. Express gratitude for all who have given of their lives, labor, and love to bring this meal to your table. Add a special bow of appreciation for the senses you accessed to make this meal an even richer experience of self-nurturance.

Savor every morsel as you would a work of art. Listen for your body's cues telling you that you are full.

Clear the table and wash the dishes with the same awareness you used to prepare and eat your meal. Pay attention to the temperature of the water, the smell of the soap, the glint of light against the drying dishes. Approaching clean up with all of your senses allows you to notice the effort and ease of such an ordinary, and sometimes burdensome, task.

Reflection

After your meal, take another seated meditation break. At the end of this period of quiet sitting, reflect on the experience. Note any differences: Are you more comfortable with the process? Can you find compassion for your practice?

Moving into Meditation

For this walking meditation, find a small area—as short as eight or ten feet—in your home or on a porch where you can walk free of obstructions. Set a timer for ten minutes.

- Begin by standing at one edge of your walking "field." Standing still, relax your shoulders; keep your back straight but not rigid; relax your hands at your sides.
- Slowly and deliberately raise your left foot off of the floor. When you do this you will also notice the weight of your body moving over to the right leg. Notice the sensation of the weight shifting to the right side. When your weight has settled on your right foot, slowly bring your left foot to the ground. Slowly and deliberately lift your right foot, feeling your weight shift to the left.
- Continue this walking pattern—slowly lifting your left foot, shifting your weight to the right foot, lowering left foot, lifting right foot, back and forth. Move through space with slow, mindful awareness of your body's movement, your breath, your thoughts.
- When you reach the end of the area in which you are walking, turn slowly, and mindfully retrace your steps. Note mentally "Lifting, moving, placing" as you do this to keep the mind focused on the movements of your feet.
- Continue until the timer sounds the end of your walking meditation period.

Reflection

After you have finished your walking meditation, sit for another seated meditation. At the end of this period of quiet sitting, see if you notice any differences in the practice. Remember, this is a practice of observation, not judgment or achievement.

Breathing Meditation

Yogis practice several forms of breathing that cultivate meditative states. Whole books are written on pranayama, which translates as controlling (yama) the life force (prana). For this retreat, you can practice one of the simpler forms of pranayama, the dirgha or three-part breath.

In this practice of breathing meditation you will use controlled inhalations and exhalations to focus the mind. If you are a newcomer to pranayama, begin slowly. Do five or ten rounds, rest, then do another set of five or ten breaths. If you get dizzy or light-headed, stop and lie down.

- Begin by sitting in a comfortable position, just as you have been doing for seated meditation. Pay special attention to your belly and relax this area. You will begin by practicing each phase of the three-part breath for several inhalations and exhalations before putting them together as one fluid movement.
- The first phase of the three-part breath begins by placing your palms on your belly with the fingertips of one hand touching the other. Slowly inhale through your nose until you feel your belly expand under your palms. Exhale and feel your belly flatten back to its starting position. Repeat several times. Focus on bringing breath deeply enough into your lungs so that you feel the expansion and contraction down into your lower abdomen.
- Move into the second phase of the three-part breath by resting the palms of your hands on the sides of your rib cage. Slowly inhale into your chest. Feel how your ribs widen under your palms. If the inhalation is deep enough, you may feel the rib cage press out into your hands. When you exhale, the ribs ease back to their resting position. Repeat several times, gaining awareness of how the center of your body expands and contracts with each breath.
- Practice the third phase of the three-part breath with your palms resting on your upper chest just below your collarbone. Inhale and bring your breath into your upper chest so that you feel a slight lift in your collar bone. Exhale and feel the collar bone rest back into position. This is a more subtle movement than what you may have felt in your belly or rib cage. Be patient as you practice.
- To practice dirgha pranayama or the full three-part breath, exhale completely. On the inhalation move your hands to your belly then to your rib cage and

finally to your collarbone. Notice how those parts of your body expand as the in-breath fills your lungs. With the exhalation move your palms from the collarbone, to the rib cage and down to the belly, feeling how these sections of your body relax as breath leaves the body. At the end of the exhalation, give your belly a gentle squeeze to release the last bits of breath then start again. After you have the feel of the three-part breath, you can bring your hands to your lap and continue this breathing pattern—belly, rib cage, upper chest expanding as you inhale then upper chest, rib cage, belly relaxing as you exhale—for several rounds. Inhale and fill every inch of your lungs. Exhale and empty completely with the slightest press in the belly when you reach the end of each out-breath.

Reflection

After you have done several rounds of three-part breathing, take time for another seated meditation. When the timer sounds the end of your meditation, observe—how your body feels, the thoughts in your mind, any emotions that might be percolating.

Chanting

Sound is another form of meditation. Chanting is practiced in many spiritual traditions. Often the chants are sung in another language, such as Latin or Sanskrit, which gives them a mystical sound. Because the words are unfamiliar, you can focus on the sounds and vibrations without ascribing meaning, further evoking a meditative state.

An easy way to begin a chanting practice is to pick one tone and sound it over and over. OM is a commonly used chant tone in Yogic traditions. OM can be chanted in a high pitch that reverberates in your head or in a deep bellow that echoes in your belly.

Try it.

- Breathe in deeply. When you exhale, breath out the sound "OMMMMMMMMMM." Form the O with a rounded open mouth then close your lips together to keep the M sound moving through your body.
- When you need to inhale, let the OM go silent, breath in, and sound another OM. Experiment with high, medium,. and low tones. Notice how the sound travels in your chest, your belly, down to your toes.
- After you have chanted OM several times, sit in silence and let the silent OM echo in your mind. This inner OM can be a focal point for a few more minutes of meditation.

Final Reflection

After this chanting practice, set your timer for a final seated meditation. At the end of your meditation, proceed to the closing Petite Retreat reflection.

EMERGING RENEWED

For both the short and longer retreats, conclude with some time to process the experience of stepping into stillness. In your journal, jot down some thoughts about . . .

> *What was the most nurturing aspect of my retreat?*
>
> *How do I feel after sampling several different approaches to meditation and mindful living—in mind, in body, in spirit? Which ones did I like? Which ones were challenging?*
>
> *What aspects of the retreat were particularly enriching? What was uncomfortable or unsettling?*
>
> *How can cultivating a sense of stillness as I go through the busyness of my day affect the way I relate to my family, friends, co-workers, casual acquaintances?*
>
> *What part of my experience would I be willing to recreate more frequently?*

End your retreat by extinguishing your candle with this closing blessing:

> *I am grateful for this time I have created for myself. I step into the remainder of this day with a sense of accomplishment, appreciation, and self-awareness.*

5

COME TO YOUR SENSES

There are two ways to live your life. One is as though nothing is a miracle. The other is as though everything is a miracle.

—Albert Einstein

Think back to your last drive to a familiar place—work, the grocery store, church. Did you arrive and realize that you had gotten there without really seeing the houses you passed and the trees along the road? If you are sleepwalking through these daily activities, a Come to Your Senses Petite Retreat is a wake-up call to the miracle of your life.

Whether you take a couple of hours or a full day, you will explore all of your senses. You may find yourself moving in closer to observe a spider busily spinning her web on a window screen. You may step back to soak up the colors, shapes, and smells of your kitchen. Living wide open gives you a new perspective. What seemed boring or of little worth—including you and your home—takes on new value when approached with more finely tuned senses.

Every day you are saturated with stimulation. Shutting out much of the sounds, odors, and activity is a protective device against a barrage of ringing cell phones, honking traffic, droning news reports, and the voices of the people who demand your time. If you heard, smelled, and felt everything you encounter every day you would soon short-circuit.

Yet the same tactics that protect you from overload can also numb your ability to fully appreciate the beauty of your life. Moving so fast and anticipating what is coming, you deny yourself a connection to the present moment. You forget to stop to smell the roses. Or pet the cat. Or savor the flavors of a meal. Crickets sing and you don't hear over the sound of the evening news.

When you come to your senses, you will immerse yourself in sensory awareness. The senses are natural gateways to mindfulness. In Chinese medicine, one definition of health or balance is when all of the orifices are open, that is, when you are aware of messages from all of your senses. Eating a meal with gusto, absorbing every note of a symphony, smelling freshly mowed grass—each act becomes a conscious interaction with your home and a life-enhancing connection to the essence of who you are and love to be.

SETTING YOUR INTENTION

What do I want from a Come to Your Senses retreat?

During a Come to Your Senses retreat you will relate to your surroundings with heightened awareness. Food, music, nature, and the objects around your home emerge from a fog of familiarity. Touching, tasting, listening, feeling, and sniffing your way through your retreat will inspire awe for the multisensory landscape of your home and gratitude for the gifts of your senses. Make a commitment that, for just a few hours, you will disengage from cruise control and experience the simple pleasures of your life with the three-dimensional wonder of a child.

In a sentence or two, record in your journal:

What I want most to experience during my Come to Your Senses retreat is . . .

Now consider:

How do I want to feel at the end of my Petite Retreat?

Pick two or three words to describe how you would like to feel after experiencing this time of sensory awareness. Some ideas . . . *attuned, sensitive, appreciative, connected, alive, energized, grounded in the moment.*

In your journal, record:

At the end of my Come to Your Senses retreat, I want to feel . . .

MAKING PREPARATIONS

For the Short & Sweet retreat, you will turn meal preparation into a sensory delight. During the Full Course retreat, everything you see, taste, touch, smell, and hear will come alive under your watchful attention. To prepare for your retreat, you will need to do some advance preparation. Here are some things to consider doing ahead of time:

- Flip through some cookbooks or your recipe box and create a menu for a nourishing, sense-awakening meal. Pick a favorite from childhood, borrow one from a friend, or select something you have always wanted to try. Splurge with a special dessert.
- Check your pantry and refrigerator for the ingredients you need for your meal. Make a shopping list and purchase anything not already in stock.
- Assemble the kitchen tools you need for your meal or borrow anything you do not have.
- Find everything you need to set an elegant table—dishes, glassware, linen, flowers, candles.
- Look over your music collection. Pull out a few CDs that can be the soundtrack or the centerpiece for your retreat. Find or borrow a set of headphones.

INGREDIENTS FOR THIS RETREAT

- Recipe, groceries, equipment, and other supplies for your meal
- Table setting: special dishes, silverware, cloth napkin, flowers, candles
- Music and headphones
- Camera
- Ears, eyes, skin, taste buds, nose

THE RETREAT COMMENCES

For both the short and full-day retreats, after you have set your intention, light your Petite Retreat candle and say,

> *As I light this candle, I commit to creating a time for myself in which I find renewal and enjoyment. During my Petite Retreat, I intend to* [restate the intention you recorded in your journal].

Sit for a few minutes and let your intention start to simmer.

SHORT & SWEET RETREAT: A Feast for the Senses

Cooking is often just one more chore for many women. The meal you will prepare for your short retreat is an experiment in turning the ordinary into the extraordinary. Whether you prepare a gourmet meal or a simple sandwich, make each step—from assembling the ingredients to savoring each bite—a treat for each of your senses. The joy of this retreat is the journey of getting to the table and the delight of what you find when you arrive.

Begin by gathering the ingredients you need for the recipes you selected. On your kitchen counter or table make a still life of the fruits, vegetables, spices, and other ingredients you will be using to create your meal. Look at the colors and the shapes. For bonus points, take a photograph. It may inspire a watercolor or make you smile when you recall this special retreat time.

Pick up one item then another. Feel the weight in your hand. Touch the surfaces and let your fingers travel the soft, smooth surfaces and rough crevices.

Smell the herbs and the fresh, ripe produce. Do their scents remind you of a childhood memory or of a loved one who taught you how to cook?

Now, bring out the tools you will need: pots, spoons, bowls, knives. Just as you noticed the shapes and colors of your ingredients, spend some time with your equipment. Find your image in the shiny surface of your toaster. Rub your finger over the hairline crack in the mixing bowl you inherited from your grandmother.

It's time to start cooking. As you follow the recipe, watch how your ingredients change form. When you slice or chop a vegetable, notice the pattern as its inner layers are exposed. Does it remind you of anything else in nature . . . a tree, a star? Appreciate the gift of this food from the natural world and give thanks to the many people whose labor brought it to your kitchen.

Inhale the fragrances of the heating oil, of chopped vegetables, of spices and sauces. Listen as the food bubbles and broils. Breathe in the aromas.

Notice something about each ingredient and each step of the cooking process. What surprises you?

Bask in the pleasure of mindful cooking. Be present to each phase of the process from stirring, washing, heating, refrigerating. Anticipate the enjoyment of eating while fully living each step of the preparation. Take your time. Nibble and taste-test as you cook.

When you come to a break in your cooking, set your table. Make this a ritual of self-care, using the same attention you would give a valued guest. Bring out your best dinnerware. Notice its pattern and color, remembering the joy you experienced when you made this purchase or accepted this gift. Rub your hand over the plate. See sunlight reflected in the handle of the silverware. Add a crystal goblet and a cloth napkin. Fill in the scene with a vase of flowers and some candles. Smell the fragrance of the flowers and the melting wax.

When your food is ready, arrange each item on your plate, paying special attention to how the colors complement one another. Watch the steam rise from the plate as the aromas mingle. Pour yourself a delicious drink in your most elegant glass. Get your camera and snap a photo to remind you that every meal can be eaten with this same reverence, even if you are eating a bowl of cereal.

At the table, sit quietly before you take the first bite. Express gratitude for all who have given of their lives, labor, and love to bring this meal to your table. Add a special nod of appreciation for the senses you accessed to make this meal an even richer experience of self-nurturance.

Eat slowly. Savor every morsel as you would a work of art—the visual appeal, the many textures, the fragrances, the flavors. See if you can pick out the different spices you used and taste the unique contributions of each one. Feel the balance of heat and coolness on your palate. Pause between courses if you have more than one. Listen for your body's clues about fullness.

After your meal, you can leave the dishes for another time. If you choose to do them during your retreat, clear the table and move through the washing routine with the same awareness you used to prepare and eat your meal. Pay attention to the temperature of the water, the smell of the soap, light dancing in the water droplets on the drying dishes. Approaching clean up with awakened senses, you can transform an ordinary task into an extraordinary experience.

FULL COURSE RETREAT: Sensory Safari

During this longer Come to Your Senses Petite Retreat you will you step off of the fast track and absorb yourself in a sensory playground. Each sense will perk up with curiosity as you expose it to the richness of your home.

At some point in your day, prepare a meal using the Short & Sweet retreat instructions. You could prepare a full course breakfast or save this sensory banquet for a mid-day treat or a midnight feast.

Throughout the day, journey through your home as if you were on a sensory safari. Every room contains delights for your eyes, ears, nose, mouth, and skin. Everything you encounter is a potential stimulus to delight one, if not several, of your senses.

Here are a few ideas to get you started. Practice at least one from each category. Imagine that you are a visitor seeing your home for the first time. Stay tuned in to other possibilities as you approach the familiar with your sensory antennae fully extended.

SEE:
- Find an object in your home—a plant, a piece of clothing, artwork—and look at it in 3-D. For example, if you choose a plant, notice its height, width, and

shades of color. Look for new shoots; prune off spent leaves and blossoms. See the sun on its leaves or the dust layered over the green.

- Gaze at the moon. Watch as it ascends in the sky, rises overhead, sets for the night. See its changing color and the images formed on its surface. Do the same with clouds, the sun, a tree, your fish tank. Over time, notice how the object changes just by fine-tuning your seeing.

- Look around and observe the colors you used to decorate your home—paint, fabric, artwork, even the book jackets on your shelves. Notice what feelings arise—do you feel energetic, restful, over-stimulated? Is there a theme or is the space an eclectic rainbow?

HEAR:
- Pick a CD of a composer or a type of music you enjoy. Plug yourself into headphones, settle into a comfortable position, and sink into the sounds. Really listen, perhaps for the first time. Hear the notes as they climb and descend the scale. Feel how the music ripples through your body. Dance the sounds if you feel moved. Tune into the memories and emotions that the music evokes.

- Tune into silence. Sit quietly and listen to the natural sounds around you. Your breath. The motor of a lawn mower. Birds singing in the trees. Your cat's purr. A fly banging against the window. Let your attention float from one sound to the next.

FEEL:
- Your home is filled with objects you have collected. Find a few of your favorites—a shell found on a secluded beach, a piece of pottery given to you by a friend, a childhood doll. Pick up the object. Explore its shape and textures. Touch it with your fingers. Rub it against your cheek. Close your eyes and let the feel of the object give you a new relationship to it.

- Step outside and walk barefoot through the grass. Let the blades tickle your toes, the dampness coat your foot. Notice the change in temperature and how your skin responds when you move into the sun and then into the shade.

SMELL:
- Begin with your body care products. Open the lids on your cosmetics and body lotion. Unwrap a bar of soap that you were saving for a special occasion and take in its fragrance. Be amazed at what you miss most days as you speed through your daily bathing routine. Ask if the scents still nurture you or if it might be time to try something new.

- In the kitchen, survey the pantry with your nose. Do the same in the refrigerator. Distinguish the dairy from the produce. Savor the pleasant; discard the rancid.

- Out in your garden, literally smell the roses—or the marigolds, the basil, the mint, the compost.

TASTE:
- Find something that you would normally munch while doing something else—a handful of nuts, pretzels, an apple, a chocolate bar. Sit and mindfully eat this ordinary food with extraordinary care. Chew slowly. Let the juices accumulate on your tongue before swallowing.
- Try something new. If you have never eaten a kumquat, buy one before your retreat. If you stay away from certain foods because you hated them as a kid, try one. Prunes are really just dried up plums—give them a chance.

EMERGING RENEWED

Whether you retreat for two hours or a full day, conclude with some time for reflection. In your journal, jot down some thoughts about . . .

What was the most nurturing aspect of my retreat?
How do I feel after using my senses to develop a new relationship with the everyday objects and actions of my life?
For each of the senses, list surprises and delights you experienced:

Taste
Touch
Sight
Sound
Smell

What part of my experience would I be willing to recreate more frequently?

End your retreat by extinguishing your candle with this closing blessing:

I am grateful for this time I have created for myself. I step into the remainder of this day with a sense of accomplishment, appreciation, and self-awareness.

6

QUEEN OF SHEBA

To keep the body in good health is a duty . . . otherwise we shall not be able to keep our mind strong and clear.

—The Buddha

Whether she was a true historical figure or a mythical legend, the Queen of Sheba is a symbol of courage, power, and intellectual curiosity. The seductive Queen of the ancient world lives on today as a woman graced with voluptuous beauty, a judicious mind, and the wiles to attract admiration. Imagine how she pampered herself. The air in the Queen's realm was infused with the exotic scents of bath oils and body lotions. Devoted handmaidens served her peeled grapes, anointed her body, and painted her toes.

How's *your* inner queen? A Queen of Sheba Petite Retreat will give you the opportunity to find out. She may speak out with authority if you give her the attention she deserves.

SETTING YOUR INTENTION

What do I want from a Queen of Sheba retreat?

First, you want to feel pampered. A Queen of Sheba retreat turns everyday hygiene into rituals of self-care. With your senses wide open, you will relish the smells, sights, flavors, and other sensual pleasures of pampering your body.

This is an opportunity to reconnect with your femininity. Explore your body and all of its womanly curves. Pay special attention to those parts that you normally cover or hide when you look in the mirror or dress for the day. Bow to your inner queen and acknowledge that you are at choice about how to indulge yourself.

In a sentence or two, record in your journal:

What I want to experience from a Queen of Sheba retreat is . . .

Now consider:

How do I want to feel at the end of my Petite Retreat?

Pick two or three words to describe how you would like to feel after experiencing a day to pamper your body. Some ideas . . . *refreshed, rested, soft, snuggly, sexy, beautiful, alive, connected.*

In your journal, record:

At the end of my Queen of Sheba retreat, I want to feel . . .

MAKING PREPARATIONS

During the Short & Sweet retreat you will soak in the tub and give yourself a mini-facial. The Full Course retreat is a day of decadent pampering with clothes and food fit for a queen. You may need to do a bit of housekeeping to prepare the way for your retreat. Here are some things to consider doing ahead of time:

- Clean the tub.
- Assemble body wash, body brush, massage oil, creams, a new razor, cosmetics, nail polish, facial supplies.
- Wash your best towels and arrange them in a pile by your tub.
- Put fresh sheets on the bed.
- Wash your favorite robe or take out that nightgown or sexy underwear you have been saving for a special occasion—this is it!

- Set your breakfast table with your nicest dishes, flowers, and a cloth napkin.
- Set out your favorite tea and a special cup, or set the coffee pot so you wake to the smell of freshly brewed coffee.
- Shop for the ingredients for the meals you will be enjoying during your retreat. You may even want to prepare food the night before so you can heat it up when you are ready to eat. Splurge and buy prepared food if cooking is something you would rather avoid during your retreat.
- Find a book or some magazines from that stack you have been saving for a special time.
- Assemble some of your most relaxing, sensual music.
- Stock up on scented candles and place then around the bathroom and bedroom.
- Buy yourself some flowers.

INGREDIENTS FOR THIS RETREAT

- Fragrant candles
- Bath supplies: scented bath beads, bubbles, oil, rose petals, herb sachets, lemon slices
- Body brush
- Exfoliating salts
- Inflatable bath pillow
- Hair shampoo, conditioner, gel
- Body lotions
- Facial supplies: cleanser, exfoliants, masque, toner, moisturizer, cucumber slices or herbal tea bags
- Manicure and pedicure supplies
- Clean, fluffy towels (Bonus: Warm them on your radiator, if you have this kind of heat.)
- A special quilt or afghan
- Flowers
- Books
- Music CDs

THE RETREAT COMMENCES

For both the short and full-day retreats, after you have set your intention, light your Petite Retreat candle and say,

———

As I light this candle, I commit to creating a time for myself in which I find renewal and enjoyment. During my Petite Retreat, I intend to [restate the intention you recorded in your journal].

Sit for a few minutes and let your intention start to simmer.

SHORT AND SWEET RETREAT: Soak It Up

Cleansing the body through bathing keeps the skin (the largest organ of the body) healthy. In addition to keeping the skin clean, immersion in water is relaxing, and floating in a hot tub frees the body from having to support itself. Some Zen students claim that a half-hour in a bath equals half a day of meditation. The Japanese say the bath is a "gift from the gods."

—Lloyd J. Thomas, PhD

This is the perfect retreat to indulge in any time, especially if clearing out family and roommates is an obstacle. Reserve the bathroom by hanging a sign on the door:

DO NOT DISTURB—PETITE RETREAT IN PROGRESS

Now, lock the bathroom door. In the privacy of your at-home spa, you will luxuriate in a soothing bath and give yourself a mini-facial.

Begin by using a soft-bristled body brush (or a dry wash cloth or loofah mitt) to exfoliate your skin and stimulate your lymphatic system. Use small strokes and gentle pressure. Start brushing at the soles of your feet and move up your legs, hips, belly, lower back and chest. Move the brush strokes toward the heart. Brush from the fingertips of each hand up to the shoulders. Be particularly gentle around your breasts. Avoid the facial area and any areas of skin irritation.

Fill the tub with water. Make it cozy warm or steaming hot. Infuse the running water with essential oils, bath salts, or bubbles. Light a scented candle or two and put on some soothing music.

Gradually ease your body down into the water, letting your toes, legs, hips, and upper body adjust to the temperature. Observe all of the sensations. Smell the scents of the bath products you chose and notice how they affect your mood. Run your hands over your body; feel the smoothness of your skin as it soaks in the water.

Soak for as long as you please. Doze off, read a magazine, sip a cup of tea, watch the steam rise from the water. Daydream yourself into the spirit of the Queen of Sheba.

When you are ready, step out of the tub and wrap yourself in a clean towel. Take your time drying each part of your body with care. Feel the texture of the towel as it touches your wet body. Take extra time to dry between each toe, moving up and into all of the creases and curves.

Apply a special moisturizer, lingering over the parts you normally skip or move through without notice—your back, your feet, your ears.

Snuggle into your favorite robe. Use the products you assembled to give yourself a mini-facial. Take your time as you wash your face, stroking each area with gentleness. Exfoliate your skin with a product you have chosen, rinse, then apply a masque. While the masque "bakes" you will have another ten to twenty minutes to relax. Remove the masque as directed and finish your facial by smoothing moisturizer on your face and neck. Look at yourself in the mirror and notice the glow.

Spend the final few minutes of your Short & Sweet retreat curled up in a cozy place or sneaking in a catnap. Feel how your body and mind respond to this special treat.

FULL COURSE RETREAT: Fit for a Queen

This retreat begins when you first wake in the morning. Wake up, stretch, smile. You have a whole day to yourself. Get a cup of coffee or your favorite tea, then get back into bed. Watch light emerge on the walls. Play some music. Go back to sleep.

Gently rouse yourself. If you are hungry, prepare a light breakfast or enjoy the prepared food you chose when you were planning this day.

The rest of your morning into the early afternoon is devoted to a full body spa treatment, beginning with a bath, then moving onto a facial, foot massage, pedicure and manicure.

Prepare for a long soak in the tub, using the instructions for the Short and Sweet retreat.

Royalty from Head to Toe

After your bath, wrap up in your comfy robe. Put on some music that will set the mood for these pampering treatments.

Facial

- Wash your face with your favorite cleanser.
- Fill a large pot (6–8 quarts) two-thirds full with water. Bring the water to a boil. Add an herbal mixture: try fresh rosemary, lavender or other herbs from your garden, dried herbs from a health food store, or the contents of two herbal tea bags. Cover and let the herb-infused water boil gently for 5 minutes.

- In a large bowl, add 8 to 10 ice cubes and just enough water to create ice cold water for a refreshing splash.
- Place the pot of steaming herbal water on a counter or on a chair so that you can sit comfortably. Bend forward, place a towel over your head and over the pot to capture the steam. Let the steam cover your face, neck, and chest.
- Stay under the towel for as long as you feel comfortable. Breathe deeply to inhale the herbal steam while it opens your pores and revitalizes your skin. Repeat several times. Take breaks between steams to let your face cool off and to breathe in some cool air.
- After the last steam, splash ice cold water from the bowl you prepared all over your face, neck, and chest. This closes the pores and stimulates the skin.
- Lie back on a couch, chair or bed. Close your eyes and cover them with cotton balls soaked in witch hazel or cold water then squeezed damp; cucumber slices also do the job.
- After your eye treatment, moisturize your face and neck with any special potions, serums, nourishing creams, or lotions you reserved for this occasion.

Foot Massage

- Find a comfortable seated position in which you can hold one foot in both hands.
- Put a small amount of body lotion or massage oil on your hands and rub them together. Holding your foot, spread the lotion all over the skin, top and bottom, and between the toes.
- Give your foot a gentle squeeze then rub your hands across the skin with a twisting motion.
- Rub the narrow section of your foot behind the ankle bones.
- Stretch your foot, widening and curling your toes, then give it another good squeeze.
- Add some more lotion to your fingers. Beginning with the big toe, rotate each toe. Then massage the toe from the base to the tip with gentle squeezes and twists.
- After you have massaged each toe, repeat the spreading and kneading motion along your whole foot for as long as it feels yummy.
- You may want to explore pressure or reflexology points on the bottom of your foot, massaging any tender areas until you feel them soften.
- Run a finger between each toe at the base and then move up to your ankle, twisting and stroking the foot toward the heart.
- End with a few gentle strokes with a feather touch. Repeat with the other foot.

Manicure and Pedicure

These simple steps can be used for hands and feet. Start with the pedicure and finish with the manicure.

- Use cotton balls or gauze and nail polish remover to take off any old polish.
- Clip nails as needed then file and shape them from the outside to the center. (**Tip**: Filing the nail straight across prevents hangnails.)
- Gently push back cuticles with an orange stick. Do not cut cuticles, as this can cause infection.
- File and buff away ridges and discoloration.
- Apply a base coat of clear polish to give each nail a smooth surface.
- Apply two thin coats of nail polish. [**TIP**: If you tend to use a clear or neutral nail color, or none at all, experiment with something bold—a cherry red or opalescent purple.]
- Seal with a top coat.
- Stay still for thirty minutes to keep polish from smudging.

Check your mood. Then dress in clothing that matches how you are feeling. Take out that sexy nightgown you have been saving for a special occasion. Lounge in your favorite, comfy sweats. Or stay naked and notice how it feels to move through your home unencumbered by schedules—or clothes!

It's time for a meal fit for a queen. You may choose to eat food that you bought or prepared in advance; or you may enjoy creating a feast just for you. Either way, use fresh, healthy ingredients that satisfy your taste buds and your sensual self.

Create an elegant table setting. Bring out the china, crystal glasses, linen napkins, and placemats. Candles, flowers, and music add atmosphere. Pour yourself a tasty drink in your most elegant glass. As you eat, savor every bite. Enjoy the tastes, textures, and smells. Focus on how this meal is nourishing your freshly pampered body.

Give yourself permission to let the dishes sit in the sink. Use the next hour or so to rest. Lie in front of a fire. Sunbathe. Curl up on the sofa. Take a nap. Spend some quiet time reading a book or magazine. Whatever you choose, give yourself time to soak up your experience.

End your retreat with some slow, gentle stretching or an exotic dance around your home.

EMERGING RENEWED

Whether you retreat for two hours or a full day, conclude with some time for reflection. In your journal jot down some thoughts about . . .

> *What was the most nurturing aspect of my retreat?*
> *How do I feel after giving myself permission to be pampered like a queen?*
> *What part of my experience would I be willing to recreate more frequently?*

End your retreat by extinguishing your candle with this closing blessing:

> *I am grateful for this time I have created for myself. I step into the remainder of this day with a sense of accomplishment, appreciation, and self-awareness.*

7

EVOKING THE MUSE

We don't stop playing when we grow old, we grow old when we stop playing.

—Anonymous

In Greek mythology, the Muses are goddesses who preside over the arts and sciences. They inspire anyone who is brave enough to commit their time and hearts to these pursuits. For this retreat, call your Muse. Ask her to remind you of your spontaneous, playful, and creative nature. Invite her to inspire, surprise, and delight you.

Children naturally know how to play and have fun. They do not need lessons to express their inner artists. As you mature and take on responsibilities, it is easy to forget the sheer joy of finger painting, modeling clay figures, or singing a tune you composed. Worries about the finished product or being judged can overshadow your inherent desire to create.

This retreat is an invitation to revive your childlike curiosity and uninhibited creativity. At your core is something waiting to be expressed—a poem, a painting, a beautifully arranged vase of flowers. Your imagination is ripe with ideas if you can suspend the inner critic and persuade the child to come out to play. Pull out the watercolors, knitting, beads, and other craft materials you have been saving for "whenever"—when life slows down, when you retire, when the kids are gone, when you are brave enough to claim a day for yourself. This is that "whenever" day!

For this retreat be prepared to make a mess. If you tend to do something only if you can get it right, this is an opportunity to step over the boundaries of perfectionism into a creative playground.

SETTING YOUR INTENTION

What do I want from an Evoking the Muse retreat?

This question might help open your mind to the possibilities: *If I could leave my fears of being perfect behind and just have fun, I would create . . .*

Take a few minutes and list anything and everything you can imagine. Tap into something that has been gestating. Surprise yourself. Your list might include taking out the easel and watercolors from the attic. You might write a poem or sit at the piano and let your fingers remember a tune you learned when you were ten. What you do is less important than the spirit with which you proceed.

In a sentence or two, record in your journal:

What I most want to experience during an Evoking the Muse retreat is . . .

Now consider:

How do I want to feel at the end of my Petite Retreat?

Pick two or three words to describe how you would like to feel after experiencing a day of playful creativity. Some ideas . . . *excited, playful, fulfilled, energized, satisfied, proud, expressed.*

In your journal, record:

At the end of my Evoking the Muse retreat, I want to feel . . .

MAKING PREPARATIONS

The Short & Sweet retreat centers around making a collage. During the Full Course retreat you will complete a mosaic project. Several other projects are also recommended, so you may want to look ahead and see which of them you want to build into your day. To prepare for your retreat, you will need to do some advance preparation. Here are some things to consider doing ahead of time:

- Find an object for your altar that evokes your Muse. This may be a picture of a person or mythical figure who represents the essence of creativity. You may also choose an object that will serve as the symbol of the Muse—a poem, an art book, a bird feather, a seashell, a sensuous piece of fabric, a stone, a piece of pottery, a CD of your favorite musician.
- Visit www.ehow.com or a local craft store for kits, supplies, ideas, and inspiration.
- Scout out the supplies you will need and assemble them in one place. The list might include: paints, yarn, glue, glitter, scissors, magazines, photographs, poster board.
- For the longer retreat, you will need materials to complete a mosaic project. Find a clean, dry terracotta flower pot (medium size), a wide picture frame, an old plate, a birdhouse, or any other base object that is made of wood, clay or other porous material to which glue will stick well. Other tools include: mosaic adhesive or clear craft glue; sanded tile grout, pre-mixed or dry to mix with water; objects with which to decorate the base object (broken pieces of pottery, dishes or glass; small tiles either whole or broken; pebbles, beads, or stones); hammer and tile nippers; and rubber gloves and an apron
- Gather together other accessories you might be using for your retreat: camera, CD player, journal, and pens.
- Clear a space where you can spread out your materials and work comfortably. Your dining room table, a coffee table, or a desk can become a makeshift "studio." Make sure you will be comfortable sitting or standing here for an hour or more. Cover the surface to protect it from your creative splashes and splatters.
- For the longer retreat you will have time for a meal. Purchase ingredients to create your own feast, or select a prepared meal that is easy to heat up or assemble.

INGREDIENTS FOR THIS RETREAT

- Altar item that symbolizes your Muse
- Collage materials for a Short & Sweet retreat: magazines and photos; glue stick or glue gun; scissors; feathers, beads and glitter; poster board or other "base"
- Mosaic materials for a Full Course retreat: object such as a terracotta flower pot or a picture frame to use for the base of your mosaic project; mosaic adhesive or clear craft glue (available in most craft stores); objects with which to decorate the pot (e.g., dishes, pottery, glass, pebbles, beads); hammer; tile nippers; rubber gloves; apron; sanded tile grout (available at a hardware store)

- Arts and crafts supplies
- Meal ingredients
- Your journal or some blank sheets of paper and a pen
- Timer

THE RETREAT COMMENCES

For both the short and full-day retreats, after you have set your intention, light your Petite Retreat candle and say,

> *As I light this candle, I commit to creating a time for myself in which I find renewal and enjoyment. During my Petite Retreat, I intend to* [restate the intention you recorded in your journal].

Sit for a few minutes and let your intention escort you into your retreat.

SHORT & SWEET RETREAT: Picture This

In this two-hour retreat, you will be creating a collage. The word *collage* comes from *coller*, French for "to glue." With a glue stick, glue gun, or other adhesive, you will assemble a collection of materials that, when viewed as a whole, will provide insights into what draws your attention, what sparks your imagination, and what brings joy into your life.

If just hearing the word *art* brings up feelings of inadequacy, keep in mind that there is no right or wrong way to make a collage. Keep breathing and have fun!

***

Time Management Tip: You will want to split your time into segments for this retreat. The first half will be used to select a focus and find images and objects best suited to the collage you want to create. The remainder of your retreat will be used to arrange the materials onto the collage base and to examine any messages your collage may hold for you.

***

The Foundation

You will need a base on which to assemble your images and objects. You can use a piece of poster board or cardboard of any size. Keep it square or cut it into a circle, a triangle or a star. You can also use a piece of wood, foam board, or any surface onto which you can paste or glue the materials you will be using. This foundation becomes your canvas, a blank slate that holds whatever materials grab your imagination.

Materials

Think multidimensional and multisensory when you gather your materials. Magazines, personal photographs, brochures, and postcards are good sources of images and phrases you can cut out. Widen your possibilities with remnants of fabric, an earring that lost its mate, dried flowers, shells, colored paper, paint, or wallpaper. If you can glue it down, you can use it to create your collage.

The Process

Surrounded by your supplies, take a minute and consider if you want to use a theme to shape your collage. You may want to invoke a quality, an idea, or an opportunity that you would like to attract into your life. Some approaches to guide you are:

- Let a question you have been pondering direct your collage making. Questions to consider are:

  > *What do I long for in my relationships?*
  > *What do I envision as a fulfilled life?*
  > *Where do I get the most joy in my life?*
  > *What do I want to attract into my life—kinds of people, environments, opportunities?*
  > *What gifts do I bring to the world?*

  Tip: Choose the question, then let it go; it will subtly work behind the scenes as you flip through magazines looking for pictures and phrases.

- You may want to build your collage around a color. If you are feeling in a red mood, look for food, furniture, clothes, cars, and other images in a spectrum of reds from the palest pink to the richest mahogany.
- An urge to experience the great outdoors may draw you to images of nature. See what animals, trees, rivers, and mountains draw your attention. Go wild with flowers, sunsets, sandy beaches, rocky cliffs.
- Take a fantasy vacation with images of exotic locales from around the world. Fill your collage with the people, sites, foods, and cultures you have always wanted to explore.

- Make yourself the center of the collage. Get some photos of yourself and superimpose your image on a person doing what you would love to do—skiing, napping, mountain climbing, nurturing a child, traveling to the moon.
- Another option is to let the materials guide you. Wander through magazines and clip whatever captures your attention.

Remember: There is no wrong way to do a collage.

After you have selected an approach, you are ready to begin. You may want to put on some mood music or work in silence. Give yourself time to clip, muse, and travel around your materials. Notice the feelings that come up as you encounter a striking picture in a magazine or an old postcard. Be curious about a phrase or quote that speaks to you. If something seems to jump off the page, it may be just what your collage—and you—are looking for.

Checking In

Before moving on to the assembly stage of your collage, take a few minutes to stretch and breathe. Now ask yourself, "Am I having fun?" If you answer "Yes," keep going. If you answer "No," take a few minutes and consider these questions:

> *Am I pushing to create a masterpiece instead of letting the process flow?*
> *Am I worried about the finished product?*
> *Do I feel silly?*

If these or any other judgments are causing you to feel pressured or uncomfortable, see what needs to change so you can relax and playfully move into the next stage. Perhaps returning to your intention might help shift you back to a more playful attitude.

Assembly

When you are ready to start piecing together the odds and ends, put aside any predetermined sense of order and perfection. Let things dangle off the poster board or keep them tightly gathered together. It is best to let the brain take a break during this stage, especially if you are tempted to wonder if you are doing it right.

Consider leaving spaces so that your collage can be a work in progress. Empty spaces also create breathing room so that your collage reflects abundance without overwhelm.

Stepping Back

Time is up! Take a break. Stretch. Walk away for a few minutes. When you come back, prop your collage up so that you can stand back and take a look. Do patterns emerge? Is your collage peopled with activity or did you choose quiet, restful images? Do you see a rainbow of color or shades of one or two familiar hues? What words and phrases did you select?

Find a place where you can display your collage and return to it from time to time. Each visit will undoubtedly evoke feelings. You will see something new or see the whole scene in a new way. Let the collage be a living vision of your dreams and goals, something to inspire you every day.

Before ending your retreat, spend some time contemplating these questions. Make some notes in your journal.

> *What did I learn about myself—who I am, what I love, what I am dreaming about, what I value in my life?*
>
> *How does the arrangement of the images, objects, and words reflect my style? Are they ordered, scattered, arranged by category, random?*
>
> *Did I allow myself to have fun? What surprises did I experience?*
>
> *What needs to happen so that I can create a life in which these images come alive for me?*

FULL COURSE RETREAT: Artful Play

For this full-day retreat, consider every aspect of your day as a creative expression.

Begin this retreat with the candle lighting ritual, then place the symbol of your Muse on your altar. Throughout the day, return to this object as you feel a need to reconnect with the creative energy it holds for you.

Releasing the Judge

The first exercise is designed to get your creative juices flowing while clearing out any cobwebs or insecurities that might prevent you from fully engaging your innate creativity.

Whether you are a writer by nature or break out in a cold sweat just thinking about putting two words together on paper, use this time to set aside all judgments about your abilities to create. Think of this as stretching your creative muscles.

Ready, get set, stretch . . .

- Get out your journal or a few sheets of paper and a pen.
- Set a timer for fifteen minutes and begin to write whatever comes to mind. No editing, scratching out, reading over. Forget about spelling, punctuation, or making sense.
- Flood the page with your worries, fears, doubts, joys, questions.
- When the timer rings, stop writing, even if you are in the middle of a thought.
- Put away what you have written. No need to read it over or try to figure it out. This sprint is designed to clear out, not explain. If you received any insights, let those seeds gestate as you move through this day. Trust that whatever doubts came up are on the sidelines as you prepare to enjoy your retreat.

Mosaic Magic

Shard art, or pique assiette, is the process of transforming pieces of a broken vase, beach glass, and other odds and ends into a handcrafted treasure.

You will spend several hours creating a mosaic flower pot, picture frame, birdhouse, or anything you want to decorate with mosaic pieces. In the process, you will create an object that will enhance your environment, grace your home, and remind you of your creative possibilities.

To begin, you can sketch a design on a piece of paper so that you have a guide as you assemble the objects on your base. Or you can use a free-form "confetti" design that takes shape as you go.

Once you have decided which approach you want to use, break your tiles, dishes, or pottery into smaller pieces. You can use tile nippers to create shapes in different sizes. For a little dose of art "therapy," pick up a hammer and smash your mosaic pieces into odd and irregular shapes.

Make sure you have enough pieces to cover your base form. Decide if you want the colors and sizes to be similar and consistent, or if you prefer to vary shapes, colors, texture, and forms for a different effect. If you are using a broken treasure whose sides were curved, make sure that when you break it into pieces, the pieces are small enough to lie flat on your new surface.

If you have an idea for a pattern, arrange your tiles, stones, beads, and other materials on your flat work surface to test your design. Move things around and break out of any preconceived ideas as you see how the colors and textures look next to one another. If you are using the free-form style, you may want to line things up by size, shape, and color so each item is easy to find.

Make sure your base object is clean and dry then start to create your mosaic pattern. Using mosaic adhesive or clear craft glue, "butter" each piece of shard and the area to which it will be applied, then place the shard on your object. Make sure no excess glue oozes up over the edges. As you complete one section, butter other pieces, filling in another area. Work your way around the object, building a pattern. Let surprises delight you.

Tip: Leave small or wide spaces between the shards. You will use grout to fill in the gaps later in the project.

Stop at this point. Allow the adhesive to dry while you make yourself a nice meal. Take some time to create the meal and savor it as if it, too, were a work of art.

Check your mosaic. When the adhesive is dry, apply the tile grout to the spaces between the shards. Using a putty knife or by scooping the grout out with your gloved hand and smearing it over the surface, fill all crevices and edges so the surface is smooth and uninterrupted. Wipe off any excess grout with a dry cloth or paper towels. Allow the grout to dry thoroughly.

Find a special place in your home to display your mosaic creation. This tribute to the Muse can be a reminder of your innate creativity—and the creative joy you experienced during your Petite Retreat.

Creative Sparks

Writer Brenda Ueland used the term "moodling" to describe the creative process as periods of "long, inefficient, happy idling, dawdling, and puttering."

Here are some other ideas to spark your moodling during a Full Course retreat:

- Write two poems to your first boyfriend or read a poem you love and write one modeled after the form and style of the poet.
- Make greeting cards from old postcards, photographs, and saved cards.
- Bring out an abandoned sewing or knitting project and conjure up the excitement you had when you first imagined completing what you began.
- Choreograph a dance routine to your favorite ballet.
- Sing along with a Broadway musical.
- Return to your childhood with a paint-by-numbers kit, paper dolls, clay, crayons, Silly Putty, or finger paints. Travel back in time as you smell the crayons and play with the gooey materials.
- Take a whole roll of film, a pack of Polaroids, or a series of digital photographs of a familiar object or area in your home from many different perspectives—up close, far away, from the top, down below.

- Mix up magic in the kitchen. Bake bread, make and decorate a cake, recreate your grandmother's special pie recipe.
- Write a short story about a childhood memory—a birthday party, your first pet, an influential teacher, your best friend, a game or sport you loved to play. Fill the story with people, smells, tastes, colors, sounds, and feelings.
- Start a Dream Journal. Fill it with lists of all of the things you dream of creating in your life—relationships, career opportunities, travel, and accomplishments. Fantasize and dream big! Begin to design an action plan for one of these dreams by journaling about what one step you can take now to bring this dream into your life. Imagine it, then schedule when you will take the first step.
- Look back on your life as your ninety-year-old self and recount your proudest moments (even the ones that have not yet occurred.) Record and post them as a reminder of what your life could hold.
- Use a kit or crafts book to make something—a candle, pot holder, tissue paper flowers.
- Arrange a basket of fresh flowers.

Remember this is about having FUN! Make a mess. Reconnect with forgotten pleasures. Experiment with things you thought were too hard, too time-consuming, or beyond your ability.

Throughout your Full Course retreat, stop and take a break from time to time. Stretch, nap, snack. Evoke the Muse with inspiring music. Play and have fun!

EMERGING RENEWED

Whether you retreat for two hours or a full day, conclude with some time for reflection. In your journal jot down some thoughts about . . .

What surprises did I discover as I played with creative expression?
How do I feel after allowing myself to play with no expectations about outcome?
What part of my experience would I be willing to recreate more frequently?

End your retreat by extinguishing your candle with this closing blessing:

I am grateful for this time I have created for myself. I step into the remainder of this day with a sense of accomplishment, appreciation, and self-awareness.

8

Two Thumbs Up

Life begets life. Energy creates energy. It is by spending oneself that one becomes rich.

—Sarah Bernhardt

When was the last time you used the *F* word? That's right: FUN! If it's been so long that you have forgotten how to spell it, A Two Thumbs Up Petite Retreat may help put fun back into your vocabulary.

For this retreat, entertainment and fun are synonymous. The first step to prepare for this retreat is to give yourself permission to sit back and be a self-indulgent audience of one.

Looking around at the piles of undone chores, you may wonder, "Is it really OK to read a book or watch a video in the middle of the afternoon?" The Two Thumbs Up answer is, "Absolutely!"

This retreat is an opportunity to step out of the role of caregiver, planner, and achiever. Pull up a chair and let someone else make you laugh, cry, or wonder.

What comes to mind when you think of entertainment? The list of entertainment options is personal and changeable depending on your mood. Entertainment often begins with some outside stimulus and makes you feel giddy just thinking about it.

Perhaps you are drawn to an activity with no redeeming value—games of solitaire on the computer, mind-stretching puzzles, hours on the couch with a book, or laughing at a Marx Brothers movie.

SETTING YOUR INTENTION

What do I want from a Two Thumbs Up retreat?

Begin by making a list of everything that comes to mind when you think about being entertained in your home. You may have to think back to a time when life was simpler, a time when having fun for its own sake seemed perfectly natural. Write down everything and anything that brings you joy when you let yourself succumb to pure fun.

Now, look over your list and see if a theme emerges. Is there one type of activity that comes up over and over—reading, movies, games? Are there different activities that satisfy you when you are in different moods? Perhaps when you are feeling blue, a good cry is just what you need. Feeling heavy and serious from carrying so many responsibilities? A belly laugh may lift your spirits. Scattered and unfocused? Something that requires your undivided attention might help you get recentered.

Use your journal to set your intention by answering:

What I want to experience during my Two Thumbs Up retreat is . . .

Now consider,

How do I want to feel at the end of my Petite Retreat?

Pick two or three words to describe how you would like to feel after experiencing a day during which you submerge yourself in entertainment. Some ideas . . . *delighted, lighter, relaxed, joyful, silly, stimulated, rested.*

In your journal, write:

At the end of my Two Thumbs Up retreat, I want to feel . . .

MAKING PREPARATIONS

Your Short & Sweet retreat is two hours of decadent play—with a book, a pile of magazines, music, a puzzle. Your Full Course retreat is cinema-therapy—a day immersed in movies. To prepare for your retreat, you will need to do some advance preparation. Here are some things to consider doing ahead of time:

- Build a "nest," a comfy place where you can stretch out or curl up. This may be a sofa, a bed, a fluffy chair. You can spread a comforter out on the floor with piles of pillows. Make space to surround yourself with the ingredients you will want nearby—food, blankets, books, videos, games.
- Stock up on snacks and any other ingredients you will need for meals. Take a break from cooking and have plenty of prepared treats available. Perhaps you will order a pizza or Chinese food to be delivered at a time you choose.
- Test your equipment. Make sure the TV, video, DVD and CD players, film or slide projector, and any other equipment you need are in working order.
- Make a list of books, movies, or music you want to enjoy. Get recommendations from friends, online, and from reviews in newspapers and magazines. Rent or borrow videos, DVDs, books, CDs. The library, video rental store, friends, NetFlix, and other movie websites listed in the **Resources** section of this book are great places to find what you need. If you already have your preferred form of entertainment sitting around the house, collect everything and put it in your nest area.
- Dig out your home movies, photo albums, and old letters. Put them near your nest so they are handy.
- Plan your wardrobe for your retreat. You may want to lounge in your pajamas or sweats, or dress for the occasion—something frilly, something exotic, depending on your mood.

INGREDIENTS FOR THIS RETREAT

- Videos, books, music, magazines
- Food for meals and snacks
- Photo albums, home movies, slides from a vacation or special occasion
- Games and puzzles
- Clothes that fit the mood of your day

THE RETREAT COMMENCES

For both the two-hour and the full-day retreats, after you have set your intention, light your Petite Retreat candle and say,

> *As I light this candle, I commit to creating a time for myself in which I find renewal and enjoyment. During my Petite Retreat, I intend* to [restate the intention you recorded in your journal].

Sit for a few minutes and let your intention come into focus.

SHORT & SWEET RETREAT: Fun-Fest

Pick from the following list to design your two-hour retreat. If you think you couldn't possibly do just one thing for that long, give it a try. Wallow in the luxury of nothing to do but have fun.

- Sit with a pile of magazines that has been collecting dust, waiting for just the right time. This is it! By the end of the two hours you may have a donation for the recycling bin, a sense of accomplishment, some clipped recipes . . . and ideas for another Petite Retreat.
- Pick a video that fits your mood or reflects an attitude you want to cultivate. Go for romance, comedy, history, documentary, sci-fi, even cartoons. Snuggle in your nest with popcorn and other treats. Bring a box of tissues . . . just in case.
- Listen to music as loud as you like. Pick Beethoven or Van Halen, it doesn't matter. Crank it up and let yourself resonate with the rhythms.
- Pull out those old home movies, slides, or photo albums. Relive your childhood or a favorite vacation. Remember fondly your prom, a wedding, even a disastrous family reunion.
- Take out that box where you have been storing old letters and cards. Read them again. Listen to the stories, hear the compliments, relive the memories.
- Get the beautiful art books off the shelf and go on an at-home gallery tour.
- Play a game. If your love of video games, solitaire, or free cell seems like a shameful indulgence, then indulge to your heart's delight. Tease your brain with a jigsaw puzzle, crosswords, word search, or Sudoku. Dust off the old 8-ball and see what advice it offers your playful spirit. Tiddlywinks, jacks, jumping rope—all games for one and for fun.

FULL COURSE RETREAT: Glued to the Tube

For your full-day retreat your prescription for fun deficit disorder is cinematherapy. Yes, a day at the movies.

The possibilities are limited only by your access to a supply of videos. Begin by selecting films in a genre. Some ideas are:

- Romance
- Classics
- Foreign films
- Musicals
- Westerns

- Comedies
- Horror
- Mysteries
- Documentaries

Another approach is to immerse yourself in Academy Award winners, the work of one director, or films that feature your favorite actor.

Animated films, classic cartoons, and videos of television series can also boost the entertainment quotient for this retreat.

Secretly hooked on soap operas? Program your video recorder and tape a week's worth just for this special retreat. You'll be alone—no one will know!

Since you will be spending a day with the stars, you may want to dress and dine the part. For example, if you want to experience a day of romance, create a romantic environment for your movie viewing. Decorate with fresh flowers. Sip tea from a china cup or set out a crystal goblet for a bubbly beverage. Eat sensuous foods—chocolate-covered strawberries and smoked salmon. Take out that sexy nightgown and feel as desirable as the on-screen starlets with whom you will share your home.

A day of foreign films might go well with Chinese take-out or a pasta feast. You can also recreate a drive-in movie setting with popcorn, peanuts, hot dogs, soda, and sweet treats. Anything goes, as long as you feel indulged and just a tad decadent.

EMERGING RENEWED

Whether you retreat for two hours or a full day, conclude with some time for reflection. In your journal jot down some thoughts about . . .

What was the most enjoyable aspect of my retreat?
How do I feel after allowing myself to be entertained?
What part of my experience would I be willing to recreate more frequently?

End your retreat by extinguishing your candle with this closing blessing:

I am grateful for this time I have created for myself. I step into the remainder of this day with a sense of accomplishment, appreciation, and self-awareness.

9

Just Doing It

One cannot collect all the beautiful shells on the beach. One can collect only a few, and they are more beautiful if they are few.
—Anne Morrow Lindbergh, *Gift from the Sea*

Many women told us that they have no time for something as self-indulgent as a Petite Retreat. The most common excuse: "I have too many things I need to do in my house before I could even consider doing a retreat there!"

When pressed to identify what needs to be done before they can take time for themselves, women recite their project lists. They have to clean out an overcrowded closet, organize shoe boxes full of photographs, iron, mend, paint, cook, clean, weed . . . the lists were varied and long.

A Just Doing It retreat may be the perfect way to combine business with pleasure. It can serve both the multitasking achiever and the perennial procrastinator. Yes, you will get things accomplished. And you will learn how to break through overwhelm into action. This retreat encourages you to approach chores with a dash of mindfulness, playfulness, and gratitude. Done in this spirit, even cleaning out the refrigerator can be a renewing experience.

Setting a reasonable goal is the first step in transforming drudgery into accomplishment. Keeping a positive attitude is another key ingredient for a Just Doing It retreat. This is an opportunity to look with new eyes at the piles you have tripped over and chores you have avoided for so long they seem like part of the family.

One way of overcoming your resistance to a dreaded task is to imagine how you will feel when it is completed. For example, you may be dreaming of a day when you can lounge with a juicy novel. You tell yourself that first you really should tackle that closet full of outdated winter clothes. Can you reframe your "should" by seeing the reward? By cleaning out that closet you not only pass on unused clothing to others in need, you are unburdened of a guilt that keeps you from enjoying an afternoon on the couch.

SETTING YOUR INTENTION

What do I want from a Just Doing It retreat?

The intention of a Just Doing It Petite Retreat can be to reduce clutter, eliminate petty annoyances, or complete undone projects so that you can feel more energetic and relaxed in your home.

A Just Doing It retreat is an opportunity to make space for inner peace, order, and a simpler life. During this retreat you will take stock of the many ways undone chores have sapped your energy and clogged your calendar so that there is nothing left for the people and activities you want more of in your life.

This retreat is designed to support you as you take some tangible, positive steps toward creating a nurturing, beautiful environment in your home. Remember to pace yourself; enjoy the process and the result.

In a sentence or two, record in your journal:

What I want most to experience during my Just Doing It retreat is . . .

Now consider:

How do I want to feel at the end of my Petite Retreat?

Pick two or three words to describe how you would like to feel after getting organized and tackling something on your "To Do" list. Some ideas . . . *satisfied, lighter, refreshed, accomplished, focused, proud, grateful, abundant, prepared, organized.*

In your journal, record:

At the end of my Just Doing It retreat, I want to feel . . .

MAKING PREPARATIONS

The Short & Sweet retreat will take you through an exercise of identifying all of the things that you are tolerating in your life, from bad hair to unfulfilling relationships. Getting them down on paper is the first step to getting them out of your way. During the Full Course retreat you will give your bedroom closet a face-lift.

To prepare for these retreats, you will need to do some advance preparation. Here are some things to consider doing ahead of time:

- Pick a closet in your home that is in need of a makeover. Start with one that you use everyday, such as your bedroom closet.
- Assemble some boxes, bags, or containers in which to collect the items that can be donated, sold, or stored. Invest in well-sealed containers for off-season clothes and easily accessible boxes or baskets for items you will store in the closet for regular use.
- For your closet, anticipate if some rearrangement of the shelves and hooks will be needed. If so, make a trip to the home improvement store to get the supplies you will need, such as a closet organizing kit. Make sure you have the tools required to install hangers and hooks.
- This might be a good time to dump the tangled and misshapen wire hangers and invest in a more clothes-friendly plastic or padded style.
- Decide in advance what type of meal you will treat yourself to for the full day retreat. Plan something easy, such as a prepared entrée from a local deli, something already frozen that you can easily re-heat, or a light salad or sandwich that will require little preparation on the day of your retreat.
- Select music that will inspire you to stay energized—and courageous—as you face your tasks. A Wagner opera or Motown dance music might keep you moving and motivated.

INGREDIENTS FOR THE RETREAT

- Bags, boxes, and containers for recycling and storage
- Hangers, hooks
- Tools for installation
- Food for a meal
- Music
- Notebook and pen
- Cleaning supplies: bucket, water, rags, gentle detergent
- Shelf paper

THE RETREAT COMMENCES

For both the short and full-day retreats, after you have set your intention, light your Petite Retreat candle and say,

> *As I light this candle, I commit to creating a time for myself in which I find renewal and enjoyment. During my Petite Retreat, I intend to* [restate the intention you recorded in your journal].

Sit for a few minutes and let your intention set the tone for your retreat.

SHORT & SWEET RETREAT: *What Are You Putting Up With?*

You will answer this question in at least fifty ways during this short Just Doing It retreat. If you are like most people, you have at least three hundred things in your life that pluck your nerves. They can be nagging annoyances or major hassles. You have learned to work around most of them. A dripping faucet or a desk piled high with papers can test your patience. Left unattended, they also drain your energy reserves.

For this exercise, think of the items on your ever-growing "To Do" list as *tolerations*. That's not the same as tolerance; in many contexts tolerating differences and conflicts is admirable. You want to respect the opinions of others and stay open to the possibility of new experiences. It's when lingering nuisances turn into energy vampires that you know you're looking at a toleration.

Think about tolerations as debts. They require your time, attention, emotional energy, and sometimes money. Depending on how long a list of tolerations you have accumulated, you may be investing your precious resources in places that are not satisfying or nurturing for you and your home. When a new opportunity comes along that sounds exciting—a trip to India or a walk in the woods—you decline because you are too busy, tired, generally overdrawn.

To begin your short retreat, get out a pad of paper and your favorite pen. Get comfortable. You may want to brew yourself a cup of tea and turn on some music. It's time to take an accounting of the tolerations that are draining the joy from your life.

Brain Dump

Number a piece of paper from 1 to 50. Without thinking too hard, do a quick brain dump. Take about twenty minutes and list anything that is not quite up to your standards. Go fast. Your gut reaction will tell you when you have hit on a real toleration. Making this list is an important step. Once they are on paper, your tolerations get out of your head and into view. Seeing them in black-and-white is the first step to getting them handled.

If you get stuck, let yourself bitch and moan a little. Paraphrase a line from the movie *Network* and chant, "I'm mad as hell and I'm not going to tolerate it anymore!" If you still have space or want to expand your list, take a walk around your house; look up, down, all around in corners, closets, and outside. Be sure to look in the mirror, too.

Need more help? Here are a few categories and memory joggers to get you thinking.

Self-care: hair style, hair color, weight, cosmetics, nutritional value and satisfaction of your diet, exercise routine, skin care, condition of wardrobe, driver's license photo

Finances: balance of income to expenses, debt, savings, tax obligations, salary in relation to effort expended, satisfaction with bank and other financial advisors, retirement plans, estate plans, wills, and insurance (or lack thereof)

Car: repair status, condition of the interior and exterior, amount of clutter, comfort of ride, expense to maintain

Home: inventory each room inside the house and around the yard; make of list of everything that needs repair, paint, or relocation to the landfill or a thrift shop

Relationships: unanswered correspondence, unreturned phone calls, invitations or RSVPs, unaddressed grievances, overdue acknowledgments, habits of others (knuckle cracking, leaving the toilet seat up, talking without listening)

Chores: meal preparation, house cleaning, taking out the trash, laundry, walking and feeding pets, yardwork

Paperwork: unfiled piles, unread magazines, teetering stacks of books, unopened mail, overloaded filing cabinets, outdated records

Computer: maxed out inbox, unorganized documents and folders, dirty keyboard, dusty screen, sluggish response time

WHEW! How does that feel to have all of those pesky tolerations in plain sight? Relieved? Overwhelmed? Clueless about what to do next? Take heart. You have begun the first step to reclaiming your time and energy. Now, take a stretch break and celebrate your courage.

Bringing Order to Chaos

The next step is to prioritize your list. Using the 1, 2, 3 approach, give each item on your list a number:

1—little things that require a short amount of time, little or no money, and, when complete, will show immediate results
2—items for which you will need to do some planning and that will take more than a couple of hours to complete
3—chores that may require help from a professional, some research to help you make good decisions, or extended time and investment in resources to complete

Moving into Action

For the remainder of this short retreat, you will focus on two items on your list. Pick something you rated a 1 that you can do in less than thirty minutes. Then pick another item that you rated a 3.

Put aside the #1 item for now while you focus on the larger project.

Using the #3 item you selected, you will break down this large task into its smaller components. You may have found that it's easy to put things off because they seem too complex. The trick to overcoming complexity is to divide the project into smaller, manageable steps.

For the project you selected, examine what needs to be done; list each and every step required to transform the toleration to a satisfier. For example, for "Paint the guest bedroom," some steps might be:

- Visit paint stores to get color samples
- Select a color
- Get help
- Repair holes in the wall
- Remove or cover all furniture
- Toss unusable clutter
- Prime and paint the walls and woodwork
- Donate comforter to the thrift shop
- Buy new linens and curtains
- Clean windows
- Clean rug
- Rearrange furniture in repainted room

After making your list, decide what needs to be done first—perhaps dealing with clutter—then put all of the other steps in sequential order. Assign a date to each step and record these dates on your calendar. You will leave your retreat with an action plan that you can follow one step at a time to completion.

Now, go back to the small project you selected from your list. For example, a toleration on your #1 list may be "dirty bathroom tub." Grab your cleaning supplies and make that tub shine. As a special bonus, add on another twenty minutes and end your retreat with a soak in the tub.

TIP: Display your list of tolerations in a place where you will see them regularly. Getting this list out of your head and onto paper frees up energy to move you forward. Use a colored highlighter to mark off each task when it is complete. Enjoy the emotional reward of accomplishing each small task.

FULL COURSE RETREAT: A Closet Face-lift

The longer Just Doing It retreat takes you into the recesses of a closet that needs some special attention. The instructions for this exercise are designed for a bedroom closet, the one where you store your in-season clothing, shoes, sweaters, and other wardrobe accessories. The same principles can be used when doing a closet makeover in the kitchen, basement, attic, or any other part of your home.

NOTE: If you have every closet in your home pristine and organized, go back to the Short & Sweet retreat instructions and make or update your list of tolerations. Then, pick something from your list to be the focal point of your Full Course retreat. This may take some advance planning so that you have everything you need on hand to complete your project.

To begin your closet clean-up, keep in mind that it is often easier to acquire possessions than to discard them. That little black dress in size 6 made you feel young and perky when you wore it to a wedding ten years ago. Today, the same dress is taking up space and reminding you that you have gained ten pounds.

While you clean out your closet, do so with the intention of filling up your personal space only with things that reflect the fashions and lifestyle that fit you today. Everything else can find another home. If getting rid of perfectly good clothes seems wasteful, consider another perspective. Letting go of anything that no longer fits you on any level can be the ultimate act of self-care. When you open your closet filled with only things that make you look and feel good, getting dressed each day becomes a Petite Retreat. Also, you will be recycling your treasures and sending them off for another life where they will be used and appreciated.

This process of weeding out can take several hours. Think of it as playing dress-up as much as cleaning house. Put on some jazzy music to pump life into the room. Turn on all of the lights so you can see into every corner of your closet.

Remember to listen to your body's need for rest and food. Take a break for your meal and stop for a cup of tea or a stretch when the fun goes out of the work.

Taking Inventory

Make space for five piles: Keep. Give Away. Sell. Relocate. Dump.

- KEEP: Everything that you will return to the closet. Be judicious about what you place here. Ask yourself: *When was the last time I wore it? Does it fit? Is it flattering? Does it reflect my life and style?* If you haven't worn it for twelve months or if you answer "no," move the item to another pile.
- GIVE AWAY: Things you want to donate to a thrift shop or a local women's shelter or give as gifts to friends. Planning a trip? Pack a few items you no longer need and leave them in the hotel for your housekeeper as a surprise tip. Another option: Sign on to your local Freecycle chapter (www.freecycle.org) and offer your treasures to people in your community.
- SELL: If this pile is substantial enough, host a yard sale. Another money-making option is a local consignment shop or an Internet re-sale site, such as eBay.
- RELOCATE: Things you want to keep and store somewhere else. Store your wedding gown that you are saving for your daughter at the dry cleaner. That box of vacation photos can go in the attic (and on your list for another Just Doing It retreat!)
- DUMP: Anything that has outlived its usefulness—keep a trash can nearby.

Now, open the closet door and slowly remove each item, one at a time.

As you decide into which pile an item will go, watch for the emotional traps. Why are you keeping that silk blouse that cost a fortune and always made you feel a bit too busty? Let it go. Are you saving those jeans because they will fit if only you lost some weight? Give them away. Do you get a twinge of melancholy when you see that red lace negligee "shrinking" on a hanger? Wrap it up as a gag gift for a bridal shower.

If your heart insists that something must be saved, try it on. Then, be ruthless as you consider: Does it fit your body, your life, your goal of making space for what you most need in your life today? No? Kiss it goodbye.

Pack up your Give Away, Sell, and Relocate items before you move on. Label the bags or boxes so that you know who is getting what. For things you are storing elsewhere in your home, put them aside in a convenient location. This relocation project is another opportunity for a Short & Sweet Just Doing It retreat; schedule it in your date book today to avoid permanently moving a mess from one room to another.

Take out the trash so you are not tempted to salvage these discards in a weak moment.

Shelf Life

Organize the things you chose to keep. Put like items together—shoes, sweaters, handbags, blouses, slacks, dresses, skirts, belts, scarves, and hats. This second sort might prompt you to reevaluate. Do you really love everything that you decided to keep? There is still time to change your mind.

Notice if anything needs laundering or repair. Make a pile to take to the dry cleaner or to a seamstress if you will not do the job yourself.

When the closet is completely empty, get your cleaning supplies and make it sparkle. Remember to remove cobwebs from the corners and to dust the shelves. At this point, examine how the closet is set up for storing your clothes, shoes, and accessories. If you have purchased organizers, install them now. Add sachets, shelf paper, and a brighter light bulb to refresh this corner of your home.

Reassembling your closet is much like creating a mosaic. Line up your blouses so that colors and patterns are coordinated. Use your new hangers if you invested in them. Fold sweaters and other non-hanging articles and store them on shelves or in easy-to-access containers. Line up your shoes by style and color; keep the sneakers and sandals in one section, and the dress and work shoes in another. Use hooks to display your necklaces, scarves, and other accessories.

Filling in the Blanks

When everything has found a place in your closet, step back and take a look. Make notes about gaps that now appear in your wardrobe. A new white blouse to replace that silk number you are donating to the thrift shop; a comfortable pair of black shoes; a flattering pair of khaki pants; a new evening handbag. Keep this list with you the next time you go shopping so you get what you need, not what is on sale.

Just Keep Doing It

Keeping your closet—and all other parts of your home—in order is an ongoing process. When you approach these tasks in the spirit of a Petite Retreat, the chores become another way of renewing your body, mind, and spirit. Once you get accustomed to keeping only what you need and passing on the rest, you will notice more readily when your life and its clutter are out of balance.

EMERGING RENEWED

Whether you retreat for two hours or a full day, conclude with some time for reflection. In your journal jot down some thoughts about . . .

> *What was the most nurturing aspect of my retreat?*
> *What does it feel like to have my tolerations on paper and ready to address?*
> *How do I feel after letting go of things that no longer serve me? How can I practice this attitude in other areas of my life—work, relationships, beliefs?*
> *What part of my experience would I be willing to recreate more frequently?*

End your retreat by extinguishing your candle with this closing blessing:

> *I am grateful for this time I have created for myself. I step into the remainder of this day with a sense of accomplishment, appreciation, and self-awareness.*

10

SHAKE YOUR BOOTY

Physical exercise removes the focus from the abstract business we engage in during much of the day and roots us in the solid reality of the body. We become more present and come out from the inner places where we may hibernate . . . Also, when we have tasks and responsibilities that can pin us down to our usual spots, exercise can get us moving at a pace more in line with our desires, even if we don't stray too far from home geographically. Exercise today and each step you take out of your head and into the world will feel more natural.

—Daily Om (an online resource for
nurturing your mind, body & spirit)

If you are greeted by a symphony of creaks, moans, and groans when you get up in the morning, mindful movement may give your aching muscles and joints a long overdue tune-up.

During a Shake Your Booty retreat, you set aside time to explore your body as it samples a variety of movements. You can relax and stretch. You can sweat and shake. You can dance like a prima ballerina or wiggle like a tribal goddess. Vigorous or slow, whichever you choose, you move in ways that awaken and invigorate you from head to toe.

This day is about paying attention and listening to your body's needs. It may be a time to return to an abandoned practice—yoga, stretching, dancing. Use your retreat time to try something new—belly dancing, weight lifting, Pilates. See what creative and imaginative ways you can use your body from head to toe.

You may find that spending a few hours moving your body with awareness will inspire you to begin that exercise program you have put on hold. You may end the day with renewed appreciation for your strengths and compassion for those parts of you that require ongoing TLC.

SETTING YOUR INTENTION

What do I want from a Shake Your Booty retreat?

You may want to get reacquainted with a practice that you used to enjoy. Perhaps you will want to try something new that you thought you could only do IF—you took a class, went on vacation, lost ten pounds. See what your body has been longing to do behind all of the excuses. Focus less on how your body looks and more on how it feels from the inside out.

In a sentence or two, record in your journal:

What I most want to experience during a Shake Your Booty retreat is . . .

Now consider:

How do I want to feel at the end of my Petite Retreat?

Pick two or three words to describe how you would like to feel after experiencing a day of mindful movement. Some ideas . . . *invigorated, stretched, energized, relaxed, inspired, committed.*

In your journal, record:

At the end of my Shake Your Boot retreat, I want to feel . . .

MAKING PREPARATIONS

During the Short & Sweet retreat, you will practice body movement by taking a class with an audio or videotape or by dancing to some of your favorite music. In the longer retreat, you will add on a meal, a luxurious bath, and some relaxation.

To begin your retreat, you will need to do some advance preparation. Here are some things to consider doing ahead of time:

- Clear a space where you can stretch out on the floor, a "nest" you can use to begin and end your retreat and return to as needed to see what's going on with your body. In this space you may want to assemble a yoga mat, some pillows, a couple of blankets, and an eye pillow.
- Rearrange furniture, if necessary, so that you have space to move freely and safely.
- Pick out the clothes and shoes that you will wear for the activities you have planned.
- Consult the **Resources** section of this book for suggested reading and videos. Borrow exercise tapes from the library or a friend. You may even have some that have been collecting dust.
- Read the videotape jacket or preview the first segment of the tape to see what props you may need to fully benefit from the workout.
- Buy or borrow props you will need. Some ideas are jump rope, hand weights, and a yoga mat. Assemble or clear off exercise equipment you may use, such as a rowing machine or treadmill.
- Find a book or magazine on yoga, walking, hiking, Tai Chi, or any other form of movement about which you are curious.
- Select music you will use for the movements you plan to explore.
- For a longer retreat, purchase prepared food or the ingredients to prepare at least one healthy meal.
- Find a recipe for an energy smoothie, buy the ingredients you need, and get out the blender.

INGREDIENTS FOR THIS RETREAT

- Clothing and shoes
- Yoga or cushioned mat
- Blankets and pillows
- Music
- Video or audio tapes of movement and exercise activities
- Exercise props (e.g., hand or ankle weights, stretch bands, belts, straps, cushions, treadmill, stationary bike)
- Books or magazines on a form of movement
- Food for a meal; protein bars, almonds or other nutritious snacks; energy smoothie ingredients
- Water

THE RETREAT COMMENCES

For both the short and full-day retreats, after you have set your intention, light your Petite Retreat candle and say,

> *As I light this candle, I commit to creating a time for myself in which I find renewal and enjoyment. During my Petite Retreat, I intend to* [restate the intention you recorded in your journal].

Sit for a few minutes and breathe life into your intention.

SHORT & SWEET RETREAT: Get Moving

Warming Up and Cooling Down

On a cold winter morning, you give your car a few minutes to idle before racing off for your day. Your body needs the same easy start no matter what form of exercise or body movement you plan to incorporate into your retreat. A few minutes to lift your arms, stretch your legs, and twist from side to side will loosen up your muscles and lubricate your joints so you can enjoy your activities injury-free.

Most videotaped instruction will include a segment of warming up and cooling down. Take tips from these "virtual" instructors on how to build these beginning and ending rituals into your retreat.

Here are several ideas for a Short & Sweet Shake Your Booty retreat:

1. **Take a class.** Bring a movement instructor into your home on video or audio tape. Choose from yoga, Pilates, Tai Chi, Qi-gong, spinning, aerobics, belly dancing, or strength training. Tapes vary in length from 30 to 90 minutes, so find one that piques your interest and fits your schedule. Put on your tights or sweats, get out the exercise mat, clear a place on the floor, and follow the tape. Do as much or as little as time and energy allow.

2. **Excavate abandoned exercise props.** Another option for this retreat is to dust off that stationary bike, treadmill, rowing machine, or other piece of exercise equipment that has morphed into a clothes tree. Put on some music and experiment with speed, inclines, and other features of the machine. You can play with other props like a jump rope, ankle weights, and exercise bands to add some juice to an exercise routine.

3. **Dance your retreat.** Choreograph a routine to a soundtrack of James Brown funk, fifties rock and roll, or any music from an era when you felt vibrant and uninhibited. If you have always wanted to be a ballerina, put on a swirling skirt, turn on Tchaikovsky, and pirouette and plié through *Swan Lake* or *The Nutcracker*. Drumming music can evoke primal energy with tempos that get you whirling and stomping your feet. Drape your body in veils and shimmy to exotic Middle Eastern music. Shake, wiggle, twist, and flail. Get naked. No one is looking!

Spend a few minutes in your nest. Get still and check in. During this rest break celebrate your body and the way movement brings it to life with an energy smoothie or a healthy snack.

FULL COURSE RETREAT: Getting in Touch from Head to Toe

Begin your retreat with the following exercise. Inventory the parts of your body as they move and stretch. Listen for cracks, creaks, and sighs of contentment. You will receive information about where you need to pay special attention during your retreat.

Easing into your retreat:

- Stretch out on your bed and take a few deep breaths. Wiggle your toes, taking the time to feel each one.
- Slowly circle your ankles. Flex and point your toes. Gradually stretch your legs, first one then the other. Allow the stretch to travel up across your belly.
- Lift your shoulders up to your ears then let them drop back down. Do this a few times.
- Turn your head slowly left to right a few times. Open your mouth wide, feeling your jaw widen and close.
- Wiggle your fingers, circle your wrists. Extend the stretch by lifting your arms up over your head.
- Lengthen and yawn into a deep, full-body stretch.
- Roll over onto your side. Curl up into a little ball. Pull your knees up to your chest. Rest here for a few minute and feel the stretch across your back and hips.
- Slowly push yourself up to a seated position and let your legs dangle off of the side of the bed. Pause. Put the soles of your feet on the floor, then slowly rise to stand.

- Walk slowly around your bedroom, noticing if your body still feels stiff. Stretch a little more. Reach up to the sky. Roll forward with a gentle, rounded bend toward the ground.

Move slowly and deliberately into the next stage of your day. Make the routine of bathing and dressing a novel experience by paying attention to each movement. Feel how you lift, bend, twist, and turn with the actions you perform unconsciously during a normal day.

If you want to begin with a shower or bath, take as much time as you like with this step. Feel your fingers move through your hair as you shampoo. Open your mouth extra wide as you brush your teeth. Exaggerate each movement. Sense how your body naturally handles and responds to these tasks.

If you are hungry, enjoy a light meal. Pay attention as you decide what to eat. Also notice if you are really hungry or if you are eating just because it's that time of day. Let your stomach and taste buds lead you to when and what you prepare.

Spend a few moments soaking in the experience of easing into your day, bathing, and eating. Listen and feel how your body is responding.

Your remaining retreat time can be as active or contemplative as you choose. Get some ideas from the Short & Sweet retreat list. You may want to pop in an exercise video and practice yoga, Tai Chi, or an aerobics routine. Put on some music and let the rhythms and your body merge in free-flowing motions that use every muscle.

This may be a good time to acquaint yourself with a piece of exercise equipment that is still in the packing crate or waiting to be assembled in your garage. Take time to read the owner's manual and learn about the equipment's features. Ease into this new relationship as you try out one setting then another.

Your Full Course retreat is also an opportunity to read up on a form of body movement you already practice or one that you have been curious to learn. Books and magazines on the topic can give you some background information that explains the physical, mental, and spiritual components of the exercise and can offer some tips that you can practice during your retreat.

Throughout the retreat, take breaks for water and a meal. Add in a snack—an energy smoothie, a protein bar, a cup of herbal tea.

When you are nearing the end of your Full Course retreat, settle into your nest for a closing exercise of progressive relaxation. The purpose of this exercise is to experience the contrast between tension and relaxation. You will move through a series of contractions and releases, beginning at your feet and progressing up through your head. Contract as you inhale, release as you exhale.

TIP: You may want to pre-record the instructions so that you have a taped version to guide you through the exercise.

Progressive Relaxation Exercise

1. Stretch out on your mat. Get comfortable by placing a pillow under your knees to relieve pressure from your back; add a small pillow or rolled up hand towel under your head and neck.

2. Place your arms by your sides a few inches from your torso, palms facing toward the ceiling. Spread your legs a bit wider than hip width and let your feet softly fall out to the sides. This is called Corpse Pose in yoga.

3. Take several deep breaths to relax your body and quiet your mind.

4. Focus on your feet. Inhale and curl your toes as you tense your feet. Lift your feet off the ground a few inches. Exhale with a sigh as you let your feet drop back to the floor.

5. Pause and feel the difference between holding and letting go.

6. Move your attention to your calves and thighs. Tighten them as you inhale and hold your breath. Holding, lift your calves and thighs a few inches off of the floor. Exhale as you sigh and lower your calves and thighs back down to the floor.

7. Pause and feel. You may notice tingling, heaviness, a surge of energy.

8. Take your attention into your hips and pelvis. Inhale deeply as you squeeze your buttocks, pull in your tummy, and tighten your pelvic floor muscles. Hold, squeeze a little tighter, then exhale with a deep sigh. With the exhale, release the squeeze completely.

9. Pause. You may begin to sense how your body feels below the waist compared to your upper body. Rest for a few breaths and let your hips, calves, and feet sink into the floor.

10. When you are ready to move on, bring your attention to your spine and the muscles of your back. Contract your lower, middle and upper back as you inhale and hold. Exhale and release, allowing the whole back of your body to melt into the floor.

11. Once again take a few breaths to pause and notice the difference between the front and back of your torso.

12. Move your awareness around to the front of your body. Inhale and tighten your chest. Hold until you feel the need to take a breath then release as you exhale.

13. Pause. Feel. Relax.

---

14. Shift your attention to your neck and shoulders. Take a deep breath and lift your shoulders up as if they could touch your ear lobes. Contract your neck muscles and hold. When you need to exhale, sigh, and let your muscles fully relax. You may want to do this several times if your neck and shoulders feel particularly tight.

15. Take time to notice the contrast between the tension and the release.

16. Focus now on your arms and hands. Inhale and clench your hands into tight fists. Holding, tighten your arms all the way up to your shoulders and lift your hands and arms a few inches off of the floor. Exhale with an audible sigh, soften your fists, lower your arms and hands softly back down to the floor.

17. Allow your arms to sink like lead weights, letting tension give way to relaxation.

18. Shift your attention to your face. With a deep breath, contract every muscle—chin, mouth, nose, cheeks, forehead, ears, scalp—into a scrunchy prune face. Hold, squeeze tightly, hold some more. When you need to let go, exhale, relax your face, and breathe normally for several breaths.

19. Let go of any muscles that are still holding your neck and head and let your whole body be cradled by the floor.

20. Prepare for a full body squeeze by taking a deep breath in. As you inhale, contract every muscle in your body, beginning at your feet, moving up into the calves, thighs, and buttocks, across the front and back of the torso, down the arms, finally squeezing shoulders, neck, and face. Hold, hold, hold, squeeze a little tighter, then release with a deep, loud sigh.

21. Rest here for several minutes. As each muscle releases, give yourself permission to relinquish all control of holding. The floor will do the work. Float in the freedom of total relaxation. Let breaths flow freely through the rejuvenated muscles of your body.

When you are ready, take a long body stretch, wriggle yourself back to movement. Roll onto one side and curl up into a little ball. Slowly rise to sit. Pause one more time to readjust before rising to complete the closing ritual for your retreat.

EMERGING RENEWED

Whether you retreat for two hours or a full day, conclude with some time for reflection. In your journal jot down some thoughts about . . .

> *What surprises did I discover about my body?*
> *How do I feel after experiencing my body in motion with awareness?*
> *What part of my experience would I be willing to recreate more frequently?*

End your retreat by extinguishing your candle with this closing blessing:

> *I am grateful for this time I have created for myself. I step into the remainder of this day with a sense of accomplishment, appreciation, and self-awareness.*

11

RISKY BUSINESS

Do one thing every day that scares you.

—Eleanor Roosevelt

Do you tread the same old path, day in and day out? Need a gentle nudge—or a kick in the butt—to move into new territory? A Risky Business Petite Retreat is a way to shed patterns that have limited you from feeling fully alive.

The Risky Business retreat is designed to take you a little closer to the edge of your comfort zone. Like a plant confined to the pack in which its seeds were sown, you may be ready to push out of a situation that feels confining and stunts your growth. Doing something risky fertilizes your next great growth spurt.

Some of the words associated with risk sound as if they belong in an insurance policy—hazard, danger, peril, jeopardy. Risky! Its French cousin, *risqué*, crossed the Channel with a more earthy range of meanings—bawdy, lewd, erotic, sexy. Add to the mix wicked, spicy, and racy, and you have the essence of a Risky Business retreat.

By the end of your Risky Business Petite Retreat, you will have met a woman you really like and want to hang out with more often.

SETTING YOUR INTENTION

What do I want from a Risky Business retreat?

This is an opportunity to daydream and fantasize. Tap into possibility without the limitations of excuses and perceived obstacles. Think big, wild, extraordinary. Remembering a childhood joy can help you step back into the fearlessness the young naturally possess. Dusting off an unfulfilled dream can muster courage to give it shape.

In a sentence or two, record in your journal:

What I want to experience during my Risky Business retreat is . . .

Now consider:

How do I want to feel at the end of my Petite Retreat?

Pick two or three words to describe how you would like to feel after experiencing a few hours of thinking and acting out of the box. Some ideas . . . *alive, stimulated, stretched, full, titillated, naughty.*

In your journal, write:

At the end of my Risky Business retreat, I want to feel . . .

MAKING PREPARATIONS

For your Short & Sweet retreat, you will daydream your way into a plan. Your Full Course retreat is a night camping in your own backyard (or some place just as unusual.) To prepare for your retreat, you will need to do some advance preparation. Here are some things to consider doing ahead of time:

- Gather together camping equipment for the Full Course retreat: tent, sleeping bag, pillows, blanket, flashlight or lantern, bug spray, binoculars. You may want to do a dry run with your gear to be sure it is in good working order. Ask for help setting up the tent and building the fire if this is something you have not done on your own before. Lay out a fire if you have the space to add this element to your camp out.
- Assemble the ingredients for a meal to be savored under the stars. You can prepare this in advance or cook over a fire during your retreat.

- Guidebooks to the stars, nocturnal plants, and nocturnal creatures might come in handy. Add a sketchpad and pencils for doodling.
- You will need a journal and some pens for both retreats; bring index cards for the Short & Sweet version.

INGREDIENTS FOR THESE RETREATS:

For the Short & Sweet retreat:
- Art supplies for a collage
- Index cards

For the Full Course retreat:
- Camping equipment and accessories
- Binoculars
- Fixings for a meal

For both retreats:
- Journal and pens

THE RETREAT COMMENCES

For both the short and full-day retreats, after you have set your intention, light your Petite Retreat candle and say,

> As I light this candle, I commit to creating a time for myself in which I find renewal and enjoyment. During my Petite Retreat, I intend to [restate the intention you recorded in your journal].

Sit for a few minutes and let your intention start to percolate.

SHORT & SWEET RETREAT: Dream Big

What would you do if you knew you couldn't fail?

This question sets the tone for this two-hour venture into Risky Business. In your journal make a list of all of the things you have always wanted to do but have been afraid to try. Let your imagination go wild. You may be surprised to read what your heart tells you. Escort your critic off to the sidelines if she starts listing all of the reasons why you could not possibly shave your head or fly from a trapeze with Cirque du Soleil.

Now, look over your list. If you have more than ten, you may want to pare down the list. Notice if your inclination is to cross off the riskier (or more risqué) ideas.

Your Top Ten Risky Business List might look something like this:

1. *Start a business*
2. *Go out to dinner alone at the fanciest restaurant in town*
3. *Take a ballroom dancing class without a partner*
4. *Audition for a play produced by a community theatre group*
5. *Sign up for an outdoor adventure trip*
6. *Take a car repair class at the community college*
7. *Get a new hair style or hair color*
8. *Take a solo vacation*
9. *"Go public"—as an artist, a writer, a comedienne, a chef*
10. *Contact an estranged friend and clear the air*

Sit with your list for awhile. Put each idea on an index card and arrange them in some order—least to most risky, easiest to accomplish to impossible. Pay attention to your thoughts and the feelings in your gut. If the critic has crept closer to whisper in your ear, once again ask her to step aside. There will be plenty of time for a reality check later.

Now, it's time to pick something from your list that you would be willing to take on. Shuffle your index cards and pick one randomly. Or examine each card and consciously choose one.

In your journal, write:

What would I do if I knew I couldn't fail?

Answer this question by recording the item you picked from your Top Ten list, for example:

If I knew I couldn't fail, I'd take a solo vacation.

The next step is to answer a series of questions that dissect the risk, assess your resistance, and move you into action.

To demonstrate the process, answers are provided for a sample risk—taking a solo vacation. The answers to the questions are guides to show you the kinds of things that you might uncover. Spend some time answering the same questions for the Risky Business you chose.

CAUTION: Your critic will love the first two questions below; this is her opportunity to tell you all of the reasons you need to get back in your box and be a good girl. Give her air time so that you are then free to move from obstacle to possibility.

1. *What are the barriers I might encounter to pulling this off?*

I do not have money for a trip right now.
My family cannot live without me for more than a couple of hours.
I have no idea where I would go.
I would feel awkward being alone in a strange place.

2. *What's the risk? What do I have to lose?*

People might think I am crazy.
I would spend money carelessly.
I would be miserable once I got there.
I might like it so much I wouldn't want to come home.

With all of the potential hardships and embarrassments exposed, it is time to move on to the juice. Your answers to the next set of questions will become the wings you may need to soar above fear, doubt, and criticism.

3. *What do I have to gain by following this dream?*

I would see that I have the courage to do what it takes to live a fully alive life.
I could visit places that are different and interesting.
I might meet people that I wouldn't meet if I were traveling with family or friends.
I might learn something that sparks a new hobby, career, or project.

4. *How will taking this risk enrich my life?*

I will gain self-confidence that I can apply in other areas of my life—work, relationships, and other types of travel.
I can take pride in having followed a dream and making it come true.

Moving from wish to reality takes more than courage. The next phase of this process is to formulate a plan that covers the resources and support you will need. The following questions help you begin to identify steps you can take to transform an idea into action.

5. *What will it take to make this happen?*

Be specific. List all of the people, information, time, money, training, tools, clothing, and other resources needed. This step will require research and lots more daydreaming time. Resources include the Internet, a travel agent, travel magazines and TV shows, friends, and coworkers.

- Decide on where to go and for how long. Research options: mountains, beach, city, country, structured retreat, educational seminar, active or restful, U.S. or overseas
- Fly or drive? Depends on where you decide to go and your budget.
- How much time to take of from work and home? Depends on the vacation you choose, your work schedule, and your home commitments.
- Budget? Depends on where you go and for how long.

6. *What is the next step I can take?*

Begin research on the type of vacation you would like to take on your own.

TIP: A fun way to start envisioning a solo vacation—or any other risky business—is to create a collage. Find images of environments, people, and activities that appeal to you. Using the steps in chapter 7, **Evoking the Muse**, assemble these pictures into a collage and see what themes emerge. If your collage is radiant with empty beaches and sunsets, a remote, seaside setting may be your ideal getaway. A scene filled with music, dancers, and food could point to a weekend in New York City or Chicago.

---

7. *Take action.*

Get out your calendar and mark off the dates for your trip.

Congratulations! Your retreat into risky business produced the beginnings of a plan that you can continue to tweak. Make a commitment to return to your notes daily or weekly and add the next steps you can take to keep moving forward.

FULL COURSE RETREAT: Starry Night

This longer retreat gives a whole new meaning to the phrase "night life." Your invitation is to spend the night under the stars—or in a tent—alone, quiet, and open to the messages nature offers when the sun goes down.

NOTE: If camping outside is not possible logistically, take a risk by spending the night in another unfamiliar setting—the guest room you decorated and have never slept in; on the living room floor in front of the fireplace; a screened-in porch or the balcony; the bath tub.

If you are an avid outdoorswoman, this retreat is not necessarily risky business. Yet doing what you normally do far away from home might take on an edge when done in your own backyard. For the woman whose idea of camping out is a room at the Ramada Inn, this may be the perfect retreat to literally step out of your comfort zone.

Begin your retreat by setting up your camping spot. Be sure that your family and friends know that once the tent goes up you are not to be disturbed.

When everything you need is in place, sit with the unfamiliarity of the setting. Notice what you miss—the sound of the TV, the ring of the telephone, the convenience of the microwave and refrigerator. With the night ahead of you, how will you pass the time?

You might want to . . .

- Get out your binoculars and look for the constellations you learned about in astronomy class. Consult your stargazer guidebook and see how many new formations you can find.
- Stretch out on your back and watch for shooting stars.
- Listen to the night sounds. Fine-tune your hearing without the distraction of TV, radio, music, and conversation: birds sing, bugs cheep, leaves rustle, airplanes and cars hum. Tune into the world that often goes unnoticed when you are safely tucked in bed at night.
- Cultivate night vision. Once your eyes adjust, you will be able to see shades of gray where at first you only saw a sheet of blackness. Make out the shapes of familiar objects hiding in the dark—your lawn furniture, the neighbor's car, a birdbath.
- Take off your shoes and walk barefoot in the grass. Feel the temperature and texture against your skin and between your toes.
- Savor your meal. You may make 'Smores on the campfire or pop open a bottle of champagne and spread caviar on sour dough bread. Light some candles and dine under the stars.
- Use your lantern or flashlight to read poetry or a scary story. Write your own poem inspired by the sounds and feelings that arise. Doodle in your journal, putting shapes to the sounds you hear around you.
- You may decide to stay up all night. If you doze or have a restful sleep, note when you wake up if you had any dreams. Record them in your journal and pay attention to the people, places, and messages that the night has delivered.

- Set your alarm for an hour before sunrise. Something magical happens as night fades to dawn. Sit with the sunrise—or heavy cloud cover—and pay attention as the colors and sounds form a new day.

No matter how—and where—you spend your Risky Business overnight retreat, stay aware of how you are feeling. If fear or discomfort arises, see what is behind it. Being alone in the dark can bring up all kinds of unfamiliar feelings. If you are sure that you are physically safe, stay still and quiet in this new interior and exterior territory.

TIP: Many of these activities can be done from inside your home if you will not be camping outside. Set up your sleeping area next to a window, open it wide, and turn off the lights to get a better sense of the outdoors.

In the morning, deconstruct your campsite with the same mindfulness that you practiced during your retreat. The experience is not over until you have put away the last piece of camping gear.

EMERGING RENEWED

Whether you retreat for two hours or camp out overnight, conclude with some time for reflection. In your journal jot down some thoughts about . . .

What was the most nurturing aspect of my retreat?
How do I feel after letting myself plan for or try something out of the ordinary and a little bit scary?
What part of my experience would I be willing to recreate more frequently?

End your retreat by extinguishing your candle with this closing blessing:

I am grateful for this time I have created for myself. I step into the remainder of this day with a sense of accomplishment, appreciation, and self-awareness.

Riskier Business

Your musings during this retreat may point out that you are ready for major changes in your life—a new job, a financial overhaul, a health makeover, or a relationship repair. Significant examination into these and other core areas may be best approached with help from a professional skilled in asking the right questions and challenging you to face patterns that undermine your success. Consider seeking the advice of a personal life coach, a financial advisor, a physician, or a therapist to assist you in undertaking any potentially life-changing projects.

PART THREE

LOOKING AHEAD: IT'S STILL ALL ABOUT YOU

12

LIVING PETITE RETREATS

Throughout this book, you have found instructions for creating Petite Retreats in your home. You may have discovered that underneath all of the preparation, experimentation, and reflection, a Petite Retreat is, first and foremost, a state of mind. When done mindfully and with intention, even everyday chores have the potential of being transformed into a retreat.

Here are some ideas for mini-Petite Retreats. Use them to bring the practice into your daily routine. Look for other everyday tasks that you can add to the lists.

STEPPING INTO STILLNESS

5 minutes	15 minutes	30 minutes
Bask in silence. Rock in a rocking chair or swing on a porch swing.	Eat mindfully without newspaper, magazine, radio, TV, or conversation. Meditate by focusing on one	Get up early and watch the sunrise. Read from an inspirational book and make notes in your

Write or recite a favorite prayer. Make a list of everything for which you are grateful. Listen to the sounds in your environment and tune into each individually.	thing: your breath, a sacred object, or a mantra such as "Be here now." Take a walking meditation through your garden. Listen to music from your religious tradition.	journal about what lesson you can practice today. Take a break with a relaxation audiotape.

COME TO YOUR SENSES

5 minutes	15 minutes	30 minutes
Listen to rain on the roof. Walk barefoot in wet grass. Dab on scented oil or cologne and sit with the feelings it evokes. Hold a cup of coffee or tea to your nose and breathe its aroma in and out. Sip a glass of water slowly and mindfully. Listen to wind chimes, a fountain, or other outdoors sounds.	Lie down in the grass and feel the sun soak into your skin Sit with your pet or an animal in nature and experience the world from its perspective. Eat a meal outside. Eat an apple slowly, mindfully. Savor the tastes, sounds, and textures.	Sit with a photo album or your high school yearbook. Find a memorable moment and relive it through your eyes, ears, nose, taste buds, and fingertips. Pick flowers from your garden and arrange them for your altar. Browse through a magazine and pick a scene that enlivens your senses. See what you can recreate in your own home.

QUEEN OF SHEBA

5 minutes	15 minutes	30 minutes
Sit with cucumber slices on your eyes.	Give yourself a paraffin foot or hand treatment.	Take a bath instead of a shower.
Write a page of compliments to yourself in your journal.	Take a catnap.	Eat breakfast in bed.
Smile at yourself every time you look in a mirror.	Give yourself a foot massage with scented oil or lotion and put on a pair of soft socks.	Curl up with a cup of hot chocolate and a book.
Put on a pair of sexy underwear and look at yourself in the mirror.	Give your hair a hot oil conditioning treatment.	Stay in bed an extra half-hour in the morning, or go to bed a half-hour earlier and listen to music by candlelight.

EVOKING THE MUSE

5 minutes	15 minutes	30 minutes
Go through your recipe box or favorite cookbook and choose a new recipe. Schedule time to make it.	Play the piano or another instrument just for fun.	Pick up an abandoned project that you started, such as knitting, crocheting, or sewing.
Read a poem aloud as if you were on stage.	Recreate a playful childhood memory in your journal. Get specific: people, place, colors, flavors, feelings.	Take out a sketchpad and paints or colored pencils. Draw yourself from the inside out.
In your journal, complete the statement: *I see my life as a work of art when I . . .*	Take out a childhood doll or toy. Play as if you were five years old.	
Peruse a book you bought about a form of creativity you enjoy.	Complete the phrase in your journal: *If I had more time to be creative, I would . . .* Make a list of things you would do to get your creative juices flowing.	Clip photos and phrases from some magazines for a future collage of your ideal life.

TWO THUMBS UP

5 minutes	15 minutes	30 minutes
Tape record yourself singing your favorite song.	Do a crossword puzzle.	Put on a headset and listen to selections from your favorite opera or musical.
Read a comic book.	Play a computer game.	
	Fly a kite.	Curl up with a book.
Play solitaire with real playing cards.	Look through old photo albums.	Watch a re-run of an old TV show.
Re-read a letter from a loved one.	Select a stack of books you want to read and put them next to your bed.	Look at coffee-table books you own.

JUST DOING IT

5 minutes	15 minutes	30 minutes
Write a note to a friend with whom you have been out of touch.	Read one or two articles from a magazine you have been saving.	Read a gardening book or magazine and start planning how you can add some new feature to your own garden or patio—a fountain, a path, plants, furniture.
Throw out something that is broken and no longer useful.	Tape record a passage from an inspirational book or several of your favorite poems.	
List 10 things to which you will consider saying "No."	Lie in a hammock and day-dream.	Rearrange a room or corner of a room.
Take your vitamins and drink a glass of water.	Clean out the kitchen junk drawer.	Browse through a box that has been stowed in the attic or garage.
Review your list of tolerations (chapter 9, **Just Doing It** Short & Sweet retreat) and identify specific steps to eliminate one.	Look forward to the next 12 months and make a list of 10 goals that you want to accomplish.	Pack a box of clothes to donate to a local thrift shop or shelter.

SHAKE YOUR BOOTY

5 minutes	15 minutes	30 minutes
Jump rope. Shake your feet, legs, arms, and hands until you tingle. Lie on the floor and do some gentle stretches.	Put on some drumming music and dance! Practice progressive relaxation. (See instructions in chapter 10, **Shake Your Booty** Full Course retreat.) Do Tai Chi at night in your backyard.	Follow along to an audio or videotaped exercise routine. Work out on a piece of exercise equipment. Design an exercise routine and schedule it in your calendar for the next three months.

RISKY BUSINESS

5 minutes	15 minutes	30 minutes
Eat dessert first Sing along to the radio, even when you know someone is listening. Call someone and apologize. Fix your hair in a different style.	Plan a different route that takes you out of your way on your drive to work. Eat something you always thought you disliked. Answer (or revise your answer to) the question: *If I could not fail, I would . . .* (Dream big!)	Pack a picnic and sit outside—in the cold! Wrap up and enjoy! Lie naked under a full moon. Move your bed to another place in the bedroom.

13

Cooking Up A Petite Retreat

Some cooks follow a recipe as if it were a sacred code, measuring each ingredient down to the precise teaspoon. Other cooks use a recipe as a starting point from which to map their own culinary adventure.

After sampling a few of the retreats offered in the preceding chapters, you may be ready to mix up your own unique experience. The following recipe for a Petite Retreat gives you the flexibility to improvise, using suggestions offered in some of the retreat chapters and bringing in completely new ideas.

Our wish for you is a nourishing banquet of Petite Retreats that renew your body, mind, and spirit for a lifetime. *Bon appétit!*

RECIPE FOR A PETITE RETREAT

In your journal, make some notes for each of the following components of a Petite Retreat. Your thoughts and ideas are the makings of a Short & Sweet or Full Course retreat of your own design.

1.   Type of retreat I plan to take
Identify the "flavor" of your retreat (e.g., Stepping into Stillness, Come to Your Senses, Queen of Sheba, Evoking the Muse, Two Thumbs Up, Just Doing It, Shake Your Booty, Risky Business).

2.   Length of the retreat
Estimate how much time you will set aside—as little as two hours, as long as a full day (or night).

3.   Intention
Consider the spirit in which you want to approach your time. List anything and everything you can imagine.

> *What I want from my retreat is . . .*
> *How I want to feel at the end of my Petite Retreat is . . .* (Pick two or three words to describe how you would like to feel after experiencing your retreat.)

4.   Possible things I will do
List some activities that fit the "flavor" of the retreat you have selected.

5.   Things I will avoid (examples: no TV, e-mail, phone calls)

6.   Making preparations
Before you begin your retreat, you will need to do some advance preparation. List everything you need to do: block off the time, prepare the space, gather the supplies.

7.   Ingredients for this retreat
List all of the supplies you will need for the activities you have planned.

8.   Emerging renewed
After your retreat, spend some time reflecting on these questions:

> *What was the most nurturing aspect of my retreat?*
> *How did it feel to give myself permission to take this time?*
> *What part of this experience would I like and be willing to recreate more regularly in my life?*

Resources

————

The search for the perfect accompaniments to your Petite Retreat experiences can be as enriching as the retreats themselves. These lists of books, CDs, DVDs, and videos will get you started. Browse your local library, your friends' bookshelves, yard sales, and the Internet to build your personalized collection of retreat resource materials.

THE ESSENCE OF PETITE RETREATS

Books

Anderson, Joan. *A Year by the Sea: Thoughts of an Unfinished Woman.* New York: Broadway, 2000.

Bender, Sue. *Everyday Sacred.* New York: HarperCollins, 1995.

Ban Breathnach, Sarah. *Simple Abundance: A Daybook of Comfort and Joy.* New York: Warner Books, 1995.

Bernstein, Arlene. *Growing Season: A Healing Journey into the Heart of Nature.* Berkeley: Wildcat Canyon Press, 1995.

Dyer, Wayne. *Wisdom of the Ages/60 Days to Enlightenment.* New York: HarperCollins, 1998.

Duerk, Judith. *Circle of Stones: Woman's Journey to Herself.* San Diego: LuraMedia, 1989.

————

Lindbergh, Anne Morrow. *Gift from the Sea.* New York: Random House, 1978.

Markova, Dawna. *I Will Not Die an Unlived Life.* Newburyport, MA: Conari Press, 2001.

Marshall, Carl and David. *A Do-It-Yourself Autobiography in 201 Questions.* New York: Hyperion, 1994.

Moran, Victoria. *Younger by the Day: 365 Ways to Rejuvenate Your Body and Revitalize Your Spirit.* San Francisco: HarperCollins, 2004.

Pinkola Estés, Clarissa. *Women Who Run with the Wolves: Myths and Stories of the Wild Woman Archetype.* New York: Ballantine, 1995.

Sarton, May. *Journal of a Solitude.* New York: W. W. Norton and Company, 1973.

Segalove, Ilene. *40 Days and 40 Nights: Taking Time Out for Self Discovery.* Kansas City, MO: Andrews McMeel Publishing, 2004.

Ueland, Brenda. *Me.* Minneapolis: The Schubert Club, 1983.

Vienne, Veronique. *The Art of Doing Nothing: Simple Ways to Make Time for Yourself.* New York: Clarkson Potter/Publishers, 1998.

Wise, Nina. *A Big New Free Happy Unusual Life.* New York: Broadway Books, 2002.

Zander, Benjamin, and Rosamund Stone. *The Art of Possibility: Transforming Professional and Personal Life.* New York: Penguin, 2000.

Poetry

The Essential Rumi. Translated by Coleman Barks with John Moyne. San Francisco: HarperCollins, 1995.

Housden, Roger, ed. *Ten Poems to Open Your Heart.* New York, Harmony Books, 2002.

Oliver, Mary. *New and Selected Poems: Volume One.* Boston: Beacon Press; reprint edition, 2004.

Whyte, David. *Fire in the Earth.* Langley, WA: Many Rivers Press, 1992.

Music

Boogie, flow, stomp, and shout with Aretha Franklin, Bonnie Raitt, Taj Mahal, The Uppity Blues Women, Ladysmith Black Mambazo, Buckwheat Zydeco, and Stevie Wonder.

Specific CDs to sample:

Dance the Spiral Dance. Ubaka Hill. Ladyslipper Music, 1998.
Endless Wave. Gabrielle Roth. Raven, 1996.
Feet in the Soil. James Asher. New Earth Records, 2002.

Groove Garden. SOULFOOD. SOULFOOD, 2000.
Kali Ma Dances of Transformation. Desert Wind, 2002.
Sacred Earth Drums. David and Steve Gordon. Sequoia Records, 1998.
Whirling. Omar Faruk Tekbilek. Celestial Harmonies, 1994.

Relax with instrumentals and soothing vocals by Enya, Clannad, Mary Youngblood, R. Carl Nakai, Thomas Tallis, Anonymous 4, and Joanne Shenandoah.

Specific CDs to sample:

Ancient Echoes. Corovaya Akademia and Alexander Sedov. RCA, 1995.
Celtic Dreams. Innisfree. Innisfree, 1997. (P.O. Box 127, Glenville, PA 17329)
Chakra Suite. Steven Halpern. Halpern Inner Music, 1988.
Grace. Snatum Kaur Khalsa. Spirit Voyage Music, 2004.
The Healing Touch: Music for Reiki and Meditation, Vol. 2. Shajan. Sequoia Records, 2004.
Mountain Light. Rob Whitesides-Woo. Serenity Records, 1994.
No Blue Thing. Ray Lynch. Ray Lynch Production, 2001.
Openings. Susan Lincoln and Craig Toungate. Dromenon Records, 2003.
Pillow Music—Natural Deep Sleep. David and Steve Gordon. Sequoia, 2005.
Poet: Romance for Cello. Michael Hoppe. Teldec, 1997.
Returning. Jennifer Berezan. Edge of Wonder Records, 2000.
Shamanic Dream. Anugama. Open Sky Music, 1988.
Songbird. Eva Cassidy. Blix Street, 1998.
The Tao of Cello. David Darling. Valley, 2003.
A Woman's Heart. Celtic Corner, 1994.
Women in Chant. The Choir of Benedictine Nuns at the Abbey of Regina Laudis. Sounds True.
Zen Notes. Shastro & Nadama. Malimba Records, 1999.

Online Resources

Body and Soul magazine at www.marthastewart.com (click on Body+Soul)
Daily Om: The daily source for nurturing your mind, body & spirit at www.dailyom.com
Heron Dance: art, words and good company for the seeker's journey at www.herondance.org
OneSpirit Books at www.onespirit.com
Sounds True audios, books and tools for the inner life at www.soundstrue.com
Spirituality & Health (magazine and website) at www.spiritualityhealth.com
Yoga Journal at www.yogajournal.com

These resources are designed to complement specific Petite Retreats:

STEPPING INTO STILLNESS

Books

Chodron, Pema. *Start Where You Are Now: A Guide to Compassionate Living.* Boston: Shambala, 2004.

Gass, Robert and Kathleen A. Brehony. *Chanting.* Broadway, 1999.

Goldstein, Joseph. *Insight Meditation: The Practice of Freedom.* Boston: Shambala, 1993.

Ingram, Katherine. *Passionate Presence: Experiencing the Seven Qualities of Awakened Awareness.* New York: Gotham, 2003.

Kabat Zinn, John. *Wherever You Go, There You Are.* New York: Hyperion, 1994.

Kornfield, Jack. *After the Ecstasy, The Laundry: How the Heart Grows Wise on the Spiritual Path.* New York: Bantam Books, 2000.

Lamott, Anne. *Plan B: Further Thoughts on Faith.* New York: Riverhead, 2005.

Lohehr, James E., and Jeffrey Migdow. *Breathe In, Breathe Out: Inhale Energy and Exhale Stress by Guiding and Controlling Your Breathing,* New York: Time-Life Books, 1999.

McMann, Jean. *Altars as Icons: Sacred Spaces in Everyday Life.* San Francisco: Chronicle Books, 1998.

Moore, Thomas. *Care of the Soul: A Guide for Cultivating Depth and Sacredness in Everyday Life.* New York: HarperCollins, 1994.

Nhat Hahn, Thich. *Being Peace.* Berkeley, Parallax Press, 1987.

Tolle, Eckhart. *The Power of Now: A Guide to Spiritual Enlightenment.* Novato, CA: New World Library, 1999.

Walsch, Neal Donald. *Conversations with God: An Uncommon Dialogue (Book 1).* New York: Putnam, 1996.

CDs and DVDs for Meditation and Pranayama

Borysenko, Joan. *The Beginner's Guide to Meditation.* Hay House, 2006.

Chodron, Pema. *Getting Unstuck: Breaking Your Habitual Patterns and Encountering Naked Reality.* Sounds True, 2004.

Maritza. *Meditation for Beginners.* Living Arts Studio, 2002.

Carroll, Yoganand Michael. *Pranayama: The Kripalu Approach to Yogic Breathing—Intermediate Level Practice.* Kripalu Center for Yoga and Health, Lenox, MA (www.kripalu.org)

CDs for Chanting

Ancient Mother with On Wings of Song and Robert Gass. Spring Hill Music, 1993.
Chants by The Benedictine Monks of Santo Domingo De Silos. Angel, 1973.
Greatest Hits of the Kali Yuga. Krishna Das. Karuna, 2004.
I Will Not Be Sad in This World. Djivan Gasparian. Warner Bros, 1990.
The Lama's Chant/Songs of Awakening. Lama Gyurme and Jean-Philippe Rykiel. Import, 1994.
Mother Heart: Songs for the Sacred Feminine by Hildegard of Bingen. Susan Lincoln. Dromenon Records, 2004.
Savasana. Wah! Wah Music, 2004.
World Peace Chants. Sean Johnson and the Rishis. Sonic Deva Records, 2005.

COME TO YOUR SENSES

Books

Ackerman, Diane. *A Natural History of the Senses*. London: Vintage, reprint edition, 1991.
Allende, Isabel. *Aphrodite*. New York: HarperCollins, 1998.
Bourdai, Anthony. *Kitchen Confidential: Adventures in the Culinary Underbelly*. New York: HarperCollins, 2000.
Sark. *The Bodacious Book of Succulence: Daring to Live Your Succulent Wild Life*. New York: Fireside, 1998.

Movies to spark the senses

Babette's Feast
Chocolat
Eat Drink Man Woman
Big Night

QUEEN OF SHEBA

Benge, Sophie. *Asian Secrets of Health, Beauty, and Relaxation*. Hong Kong: Periplus Editions, 2000.
Cash Spellman, Cathy. *Water Magic: Healing Bath Recipes for the Body, Spirit, and Soul*. New York: Fireside, 2005.

Muryn, Mary. *Spa Magic.* New York: Perigee Trade, 2002.

Northrup, Christiane. *Women's Bodies, Women's Wisdom.* New York: Bantam, 2002.

Placzek, Melissa. *Chin Deep in Bubbles: Little Luxuries for Every Day.* Gloucester, MA: Fair Winds Press, 2001.

EVOKING THE MUSE

Bender, Sheila. *Writing Personal Poetry: Creating Poems from Your Life Experiences.* Cincinnati, OH: Writer's Digest Books, 1998.

Cameron, Julia. *The Artist's Way: A Spiritual Path to Higher Creativity.* New York: Tarcher, 1992.

Edwards, Betty. *The New Drawing on the Right Side of the Brain.* Tarcher, 1999.

Fincher, Susanne F. *Coloring Mandalas.* Shambhala, 2000.

Goldberg, Natalie. *Writing Down the Bones.* Boston, MA: Shambhala Publications, 1986.

Harrison, Holly and Paula Grasdal. *Collage for the Soul: Expressing Hopes and Dreams Through Art.* Gloucester, MA: Rockport Publishers, Inc., 2003.

MacKay, Jill. *Creative Garden Mosaics: Dazzling Projects & Innovative Techniques.* New York: Lark Books, 2003.

Mastro, Linda. *Journal-in-a-Box.* Available through www.petiteretreats.org and lmastro@goeaston.net

Segalove, Ilene and Paul Bob Velick. *List Your Creative Self: Listmaking as the Way to Unleash Your Creativity.* Kansas City, MO: Andrews McMeel Publishing, 1999.

Thomas, Frank P. *How to Write the Story of Your Life.* Cincinnati: Writer's Digest, 1984.

Online Resource

eHow™: Clear Instructions on How To Do (just about) Everything at www.ehow.com

TWO THUMBS UP

Find movie ideas at:

All Movie—www.allmovie.com
Blockbuster—www.blockbuster.com
Internet Movie Database—www.imdb.com
NetFlix—www.netflix.com
Spiritual Cinema—www.thespiritualcinemacircle.com

Spirituality & Health website—www.spiritualityhealth.com (book, movie, and music reviews)

Local libraries and video stores

JUST DOING IT

Morgenstern, Julie. *Organizing from the Inside Out: The Foolproof System for Organizing Your Home, Your Office and Your Life.* New York: Owl Books, 2004.

Novak, Jamie. *1000 Best Quick and Easy Organizing Secrets.* Chicago: Sourcebooks, Inc, 2006.

Smaller, Donna. *Unclutter Your Home: 7 Simple Steps, 700 Tips and Ideas.* North Adams, MA: Storey Pub. LLC, 1999.

Online Resources

eBay at www.ebay.com

Freecycle™: Changing the world one gift at a time at www.freecycle.org

SHAKE YOUR BOOTY

Books

Lance, Kathryn. *Getting Strong: A Woman's Guide to Realizing Her Physical Potential.* Indianapolis, IN: Bobbs-Merrill. 1978.

Fitness Magazine, eds. *Fitness Stretching: Mind, Body, Spirit for Women.* New York: Three Rivers Press, 2000.

Mehta, Mira. *How to Use Yoga.* Berkley, CA: Rodmell Press, 1998.

Schaeffer, Rachel. *Yoga for Your Spiritual Muscles.* Wheaton, IL: Quest Books, 1998.

Siler, Brooke. *The Pilates Body: The Ultimate At-Home Guide to Strengthening, Lengthening, and Toning Your Body—Without Machines.* New York: Broadway, 2000.

Weight Watcher's Fit Factor: How Getting Strong Can Help You Lose Weight. Indianapolis, IN: Wiley, 2000.

Videos and DVDs

"Scott Cole's Discover Tai Chi for Beginners—Workout Essentials." Goldhil Home Media, 2002.

"Gentle Yoga with Sudha," Carolyn Lundeen. Kripalu Center for Yoga and Health, Lenox, MA. Available at www.kripalu.org

"Instant Bellydancer 1: A Crash Course in Belly Dance" with Neon. StratoStream—
    WorldDance New York, 2005.
"Personal Training System," Denise Austin, Artisan, 2004.
"Total Yoga," created by Ganga White and Tracey Rich. Healing Arts: White Lotus
    Foundation, 1994

RISKY BUSINESS

Jeffers, Susan. *Feel the Fear and Do It Anyway*. New York: Fawcett Columbine, 1987.
Bond, Marybeth and Pamela Michael, eds. *A Woman's Passion for Travel*. San
    Francisco: Travelers' Tales, 1999.
Conlon, Faith, Ingrid Emerick, and Christine Henry De Tessan, eds. *A Woman
    Alone: Travel Tales from Around the Globe*. Seattle: Seal Press, 2001.
Davidson, Robin. *Tracks*. New York: Viking, 1986.
Markham, Beryl. *West with the Night*. Berkeley: North Point Press, 1942, 1983.
Schultz, Patricia. *1,000 Places to See Before You Die*. New York: Workman Publishing,
    2003.
Segalove, Ilene. *Risk Your Self: Listmaking the Ultimate Path for Personal Change*.
    Kansas City, MO: Andrews McMeel, 2000.
Sher, Barbara. *It's Only Too Late If You Don't Start Now*. New York: Dell, 1999.
Whyte David. *Crossing the Unknown Sea: Work as a Pilgrimage of Identity*. New York:
    Riverhead Books, 2001.

Journal Pages

Order copies of *Petite Retreats: Renewing Body, Mind, and Spirit without Leaving Home* from Xlibris at www2.xlibris.com/bookstore.

Linda Mastro and Anna Harding are available to bring the workshop *Petite Retreats* to groups of women. For more information, visit www.petiteretreats.org.

Linda Mastro is available for speaking and consulting engagements focused on effective written communications and marketing for nonprofit organizations, women's life transitions, and travel as a spiritual practice. Linda is also the creator of *Journal-in-a-Box,* a kit that includes a blank journal, pens, and thought-provoking cards that reconnect you with the people, places, experiences, ideas, and feelings that make your life a unique journey. Contact her at

410–829–6511
lmastro@goeaston.net

Contact life coach Anna Harding of Graceful Transitions to schedule a complimentary session and experience the potential of coaching to create positive changes in all aspects of your life. She is available for public speaking and seminars related to reinventing retirement, relationship enhancement, and women in midlife transitions. Contact her at

410–822–6452
anna@gracecoach.com
www.gracecoach.com